GEOMETRY

Math Strategy Guide

This comprehensive guide illustrates every geometric
principle, formula, and problem type tested on the GMAT.
Understand and master the intricacies of shapes, planes,
lines, angles, and objects.

Geometry GMAT Strategy Guide, Fourth Edition

10-digit International Standard Book Number: 0-9824238-3-7
13-digit International Standard Book Number: 978-0-9824238-3-7

Copyright © 2009 MG Prep, Inc.

ALL RIGHTS RESERVED. No part of this work may be reproduced or used in any
form or by any means—graphic, electronic, or mechanical, including photocopying,
recording, taping, Web distribution—without the prior written permission of the pub-
lisher, MG Prep Inc.

Note: *GMAT, Graduate Management Admission Test, Graduate Management
Admission Council,* and *GMAC* are all registered trademarks of the Graduate
Management Admission Council which neither sponsors nor is affiliated in any way
with this product.

8 GUIDE INSTRUCTIONAL SERIES

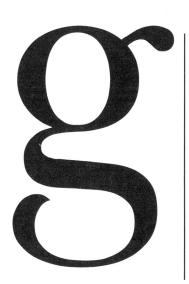

Math GMAT Strategy Guides

Number Properties (ISBN: 978-0-9824238-4-4)

Fractions, Decimals, & Percents (ISBN: 978-0-9824238-2-0)

Equations, Inequalities, & VICs (ISBN: 978-0-9824238-1-3)

Word Translations (ISBN: 978-0-9824238-7-5)

Geometry (ISBN: 978-0-9824238-3-7)

Verbal GMAT Strategy Guides

Critical Reasoning (ISBN: 978-0-9824238-0-6)

Reading Comprehension (ISBN: 978-0-9824238-5-1)

Sentence Correction (ISBN: 978-0-9824238-6-8)

ManhattanGMAT
the new standard

May 1st, 2009

Thank you for picking up one of the Manhattan GMAT Strategy Guides—we hope that it refreshes your memory of the junior-high math that you haven't used in years. Maybe it will even teach you a new thing or two.

As with most accomplishments, there were many people involved in the various iterations of the book that you're holding. First and foremost is Zeke Vanderhoek, the founder of Manhattan GMAT. Zeke was a lone tutor in New York when he started the Company in 2000. Now, nine years later, MGMAT has Instructors and offices nationwide, and the Company contributes to the studies and successes of thousands of students each year.

Our 4th Edition Strategy Guides are based on the continuing experiences of our Instructors and our students. We owe much of these latest editions to the insight provided by our students. On the Company side, we are indebted to many of our Instructors, including but not limited to Josh Braslow, Dan Gonzalez, Mike Kim, Stacey Koprince, Ben Ku, Jadran Lee, David Mahler, Ron Purewal, Tate Shafer, Emily Sledge, and of course Chris Ryan, the Company's Lead Instructor and Director of Curriculum Development.

At Manhattan GMAT, we continually aspire to provide the best Instructors and resources possible. We hope that you'll find our dedication manifest in this book. If you have any comments or questions, please e-mail me at andrew.yang@manhattangmat.com. I'll be sure that your comments reach Chris and the rest of the team—and I'll read them too.

Best of luck in preparing for the GMAT!

Sincerely,

Andrew Yang
Chief Executive Officer
ManhattanGMAT

HOW TO ACCESS YOUR ONLINE RESOURCES

Please read this entire page of information, all the way down to the bottom of the page! This page describes WHAT online resources are included with the purchase of this book and HOW to access these resources.

If you are a registered Manhattan GMAT student and have received this book as part of your course materials, you have AUTOMATIC access to ALL of our online resources. This includes all practice exams, question banks, and online updates to this book. To access these resources, follow the instructions in the Welcome Guide provided to you at the start of your program. Do NOT follow the instructions below.

If you have purchased this book, your purchase includes 1 YEAR OF ONLINE ACCESS to the following:

>   **6 Computer Adaptive Online Practice Exams**
>
>   **Bonus Online Question Bank for *GEOMETRY***
>
>   **Online Updates to the Content in this Book**

ONLINE RESOURCE ACTIVATION

If you purchased this book from the Manhattan GMAT Online Store or at one of our Centers, you already have access to all practice exams and the Bonus Online Question Bank for *GEOMETRY*. You can access them at **http://www.manhattangmat.com/practicecenter.cfm**. Otherwise, follow the instructions below.

To register and start using your online resources, please follow the instructions at the following URL:

http://www.manhattangmat.com/access.cfm   (Double check that you have typed this in accurately!)

Your one year of online access begins on the day that you register your book at the above URL. You only need to register your product ONCE at the above URL. To use your online resources any time AFTER you have completed the registration process, please login to the following URL:

http://www.manhattangmat.com/practicecenter.cfm

The 6 full-length computer adaptive practice exams included with the purchase of this book are delivered online using Manhattan GMAT's proprietary computer-adaptive test engine. The exams adapt to your ability level by drawing from a bank of more than 1,200 unique questions of varying difficulty levels written by Manhattan GMAT's expert instructors, all of whom have scored in the 99th percentile on the Official GMAT. At the end of each exam you will receive a score, an analysis of your results, and the opportunity to review detailed explanations for each question. You may choose to take the exams timed or untimed.

The Bonus Online Question Bank for *GEOMETRY* consists of 25 extra practice questions (with detailed explanations) that test the variety of Geometry concepts and skills covered in this book. These questions provide you with extra practice *beyond* the problem sets contained in this book. You may use our online timer to practice your pacing by setting time limits for each question in the bank.

The content presented in this book is updated periodically to ensure that it reflects the GMAT's most current trends. You may view all updates, including any known errors or changes, upon registering for online access.

Important Note: The 6 computer adaptive online exams included with the purchase of this book are the SAME exams that you receive upon purchasing ANY book in Manhattan GMAT's 8 Book Strategy Series. On the other hand, the Bonus Online Question Bank for *GEOMETRY* is a unique resource that you receive ONLY with the purchase of this specific title.

Part I: General

Part II: Advanced

TABLE OF CONTENTS

PART I: GENERAL

This part of the book covers both basic and intermediate topics within *Geometry*.
Complete Part I before moving on to Part II: Advanced.

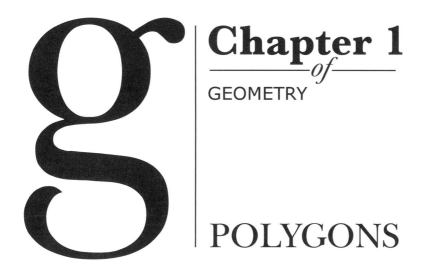

Chapter 1
of
GEOMETRY

POLYGONS

In This Chapter . . .

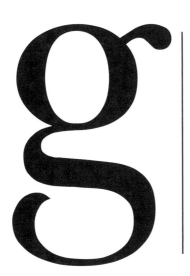

POLYGONS

A polygon is defined as a closed shape formed by line segments. The polygons tested on the GMAT include the following:

- Three-sided shapes (Triangles)
- Four-sided shapes (Quadrilaterals)
- Other polygons with *n* sides (where *n* is five or more)

This section will focus on polygons of four or more sides. In particular, the GMAT emphasizes quadrilaterals—or four-sided polygons—including trapezoids, parallelograms, and special parallelograms, such as rhombuses, rectangles, and squares.

Polygons are two-dimensional shapes—they lie in a plane. The GMAT tests your ability to work with different measurements associated with polygons. The measurements you must be adept with are (1) interior angles, (2) perimeter, and (3) area.

The GMAT also tests your knowledge of three-dimensional shapes formed from polygons, particularly rectangular solids and cubes. The measurements you must be adept with are (1) surface area and (2) volume.

A polygon is a closed shape formed by line segments.

Quadrilaterals: An Overview

The most common polygon tested on the GMAT, aside from the triangle, is the quadrilateral (any four-sided polygon). Almost all GMAT polygon problems involve the special types of quadrilaterals shown below.

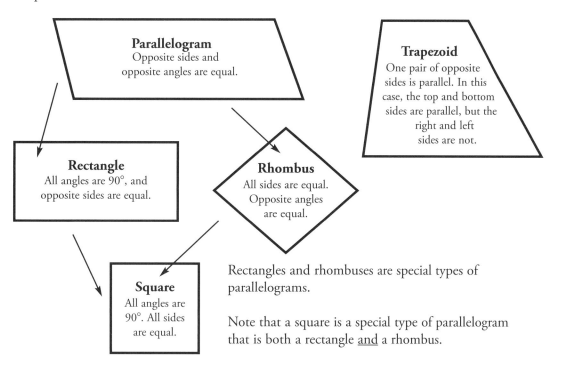

Parallelogram
Opposite sides and opposite angles are equal.

Trapezoid
One pair of opposite sides is parallel. In this case, the top and bottom sides are parallel, but the right and left sides are not.

Rectangle
All angles are 90°, and opposite sides are equal.

Rhombus
All sides are equal. Opposite angles are equal.

Square
All angles are 90°. All sides are equal.

Rectangles and rhombuses are special types of parallelograms.

Note that a square is a special type of parallelogram that is both a rectangle <u>and</u> a rhombus.

Polygons and Interior Angles

The sum of the interior angles of a given polygon depends only on the **number of sides in the polygon**. The following chart displays the relationship between the type of polygon and the sum of its interior angles.

Another way to find the sum of the interior angles in a polygon is to divide the polygon into triangles. The interior angles of each triangle sum to 180°.

The sum of the interior angles of a polygon follows a specific pattern that depends on n, the number of sides that the polygon has. This sum is always 180° times 2 less than n (the number of sides), because the polygon can be cut into $(n-2)$ triangles, each of which contains 180°.

Polygon	# of Sides	Sum of Interior Angles
Triangle	3	180°
Quadrilateral	4	360°
Pentagon	5	540°
Hexagon	6	720°

This pattern can be expressed with the following formula:

$$(n - 2) \times 180 = \text{Sum of Interior Angles of a Polygon}$$

Since this polygon has four sides, the sum of its interior angles is $(4-2)180 = 2(180) = 360°$.

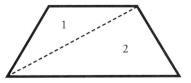

Alternatively, note that a quadrilateral can be cut into two triangles by a line connecting opposite corners. Thus, the sum of the angles = $2(180) = 360°$.

Since the next polygon has six sides, the sum of its interior angles is $(6-2)180 = 4(180) = 720°$.

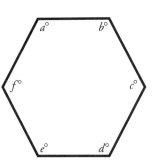

Alternatively, note that a hexagon can be cut into four triangles by three lines connecting corners.

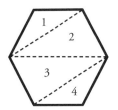

Thus, the sum of the angles = $4(180) = 720°$.

By the way, the corners of polygons are also known as vertices (singular: vertex).

Polygons and Perimeter

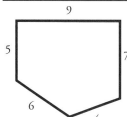

The perimeter refers to the distance around a polygon, or the sum of the lengths of all the sides. The amount of fencing needed to surround a yard would be equivalent to the perimeter of that yard (the sum of all the sides).

The perimeter of the pentagon to the left is:
$$9 + 7 + 4 + 6 + 5 = \mathbf{31}.$$

Polygons and Area

The area of a polygon refers to the space inside the polygon. Area is measured in square units, such as cm² (square centimeters), m² (square meters), or ft² (square feet). For example, the amount of space that a garden occupies is the area of that garden.

On the GMAT, there are two polygon area formulas you MUST know:

1) Area of a TRIANGLE $= \dfrac{\textbf{Base} \times \textbf{Height}}{\textbf{2}}$

The base refers to the bottom side of the triangle. The height ALWAYS refers to a line that is perpendicular (at a 90° angle) to the base.

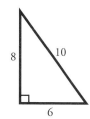

In this triangle, the base is 6 and the height (perpendicular to the base) is 8. The area = (6 × 8) ÷ 2 = 48 ÷ 2 = 24.

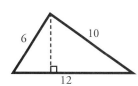

In this triangle, the base is 12, but the height is not shown. Neither of the other two sides of the triangle is perpendicular to the base. In order to find the area of this triangle, we would first need to determine the height, which is represented by the dotted line.

2) Area of a RECTANGLE = **Length** × **Width**

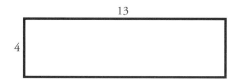

The length of this rectangle is 13, and the width is 4. Therefore, the area = 13 × 4 = 52.

You must memorize the formulas for the area of a triangle and for the area of the quadrilaterals shown in this section.

The GMAT will occasionally ask you to find the area of a polygon more complex than a simple triangle or rectangle. The following formulas can be used to find the areas of other types of quadrilaterals:

3) Area of a TRAPEZOID $= \dfrac{(\textbf{Base}_1 + \textbf{Base}_2) \times \textbf{Height}}{2}$

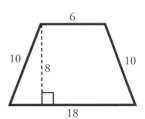

Note that the height refers to a line perpendicular to the two bases, which are parallel. (You often have to draw in the height, as in this case.) In the trapezoid shown, base$_1$ = 18, base$_2$ = 6, and the height = 8. The area = (18 + 6) × 8 ÷ 2 = 96. Another way to think about this is to take the *average* of the two bases and multiply it by the height.

4) Area of any PARALLELOGRAM = **Base × Height**

Note that the height refers to the line perpendicular to the base. (As with the trapezoid, you often have to draw in the height.) In the parallelogram shown, the base = 5 and the height = 8. Therefore, the area is 5 × 8 = 40.

5) Area of a RHOMBUS $= \dfrac{\textbf{Diagonal}_1 \times \textbf{Diagonal}_2}{2}$

Note that the diagonals of a rhombus are ALWAYS perpendicular bisectors (meaning that they cut each other in half at a 90° angle).

The area of this rhombus is $\dfrac{6 \times 8}{2} = \dfrac{48}{2} = 24$.

Although these formulas are very useful to memorize for the GMAT, you may notice that all of the above shapes can actually be divided into some combination of rectangles and right triangles. Therefore, if you forget the area formula for a particular shape, simply cut the shape into rectangles and right triangles, and then find the areas of these individual pieces. For example:

Notice that most of these formulas involve finding a base and a line perpendicular to that base (a height).

3 Dimensions: Surface Area

The GMAT tests two particular three-dimensional shapes formed from polygons: the rectangular solid and the cube. Note that a cube is just a special type of rectangular solid.

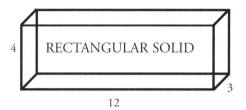
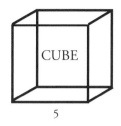

The surface area of a three-dimensional shape is the amount of space on the surface of that particular object. For example, the amount of paint that it would take to fully cover a rectangular box could be determined by finding the surface area of that box. As with simple area, surface area is measured in square units such as inches^2 (square inches) or ft^2 (square feet).

> **Surface Area = the SUM of the areas of ALL of the faces**

Both a rectangular solid and a cube have **six faces**.

To determine the surface area of a rectangular solid, you must find the area of each face. Notice, however, that in a rectangular solid, the front and back faces have the same area, the top and bottom faces have the same area, and the two side faces have the same area. In the solid above, the area of the front face is equal to $12 \times 4 = 48$. Thus, the back face also has an area of 48. The area of the bottom face is equal to $12 \times 3 = 36$. Thus, the top face also has an area of 36. Finally, each side face has an area of $3 \times 4 = 12$. Therefore, the surface area, or the sum of the areas of all six faces equals $48(2) + 36(2) + 12(2) = 192$.

To determine the surface area of a cube, you only need the length of one side. We can see from the cube above that a cube is made of six square surfaces. First, find the area of one face: $5 \times 5 = 25$. Then, multiply by six to account for all of the faces: $6 \times 25 = 150$.

You do not need to memorize a formula for surface area. Simply find the sum of all of the faces.

3 Dimensions: Volume

The volume of a three-dimensional shape is the amount of "stuff" it can hold. "Capacity" is another word for volume. For example, the amount of liquid that a rectangular milk carton holds can be determined by finding the volume of the carton. Volume is measured in cubic units such as inches^3 (cubic inches), ft^3 (cubic feet), or m^3 (cubic meters).

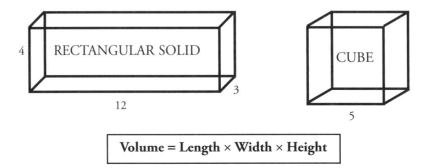

Another way to think about this formula is that the volume is equal to the area of the base multiplied by the height.

$$\textbf{Volume = Length} \times \textbf{Width} \times \textbf{Height}$$

By looking at the rectangular solid above, we can see that the length is 12, the width is 3, and the height is 4. Therefore, the volume is $12 \times 3 \times 4 = 144$.

In a cube, all three of the dimensions—length, width, and height—are identical. Therefore, knowing the measurement of just one side of the cube is sufficient to find the volume. In the cube above, the volume is $5 \times 5 \times 5 = 125$.

Beware of a GMAT volume trick:

> How many books, each with a volume of 100 in^3, can be packed into a crate with a volume of 5,000 in^3?

It is tempting to answer "50 books" (since $50 \times 100 = 5,000$). However, this is incorrect, because we do not know the exact dimensions of each book! One book might be $5 \times 5 \times 4$, while another book might be $20 \times 5 \times 1$. Even though both have a volume of 100 in^3, they have different rectangular shapes. Without knowing the exact shapes of all the books, we cannot tell whether they would all fit into the crate. Remember, when you are fitting 3-dimensional objects into other 3-dimensional objects, knowing the respective volumes is not enough. We must know the specific dimensions (length, width, and height) of each object to determine whether the objects can fit without leaving gaps.

Problem Set (Note: Figures are not drawn to scale.)

1. Frank the Fencemaker needs to fence in a rectangular yard. He fences in the entire yard, except for one 40-foot side of the yard. The yard has an area of 280 square feet. How many feet of fence does Frank use?

2. A pentagon has three sides with length x, and two sides with the length $3x$. If x is $\frac{2}{3}$ of an inch, what is the perimeter of the pentagon?

3. ABCD is a quadrilateral, with AB parallel to CD (see figure). E is a point between C and D such that AE represents the height of ABCD, and E is the midpoint of CD. If AB is 4 inches long, AE is 5 inches long, and the area of triangle AED is 12.5 square inches, what is the area of ABCD?

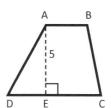

4. A rectangular tank needs to be coated with insulation. The tank has dimensions of 4 feet, 5 feet, and 2.5 feet. Each square foot of insulation costs $20. How much will it cost to cover the surface of the tank with insulation?

5. Triangle ABC (see figure) has a base of $2y$, a height of y, and an area of 49. What is y?

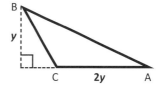

6. 40 percent of Andrea's living room floor is covered by a carpet that is 4 feet by 9 feet. What is the area of her living room floor?

7. If the perimeter of a rectangular flower bed is 30 feet, and its area is 44 square feet, what is the length of each of its shorter sides?

8. There is a rectangular parking lot with a length of $2x$ and a width of x. What is the ratio of the perimeter of the parking lot to the area of the parking lot, in terms of x?

9. A rectangular solid has a square base, with each side of the base measuring 4 meters. If the volume of the solid is 112 cubic meters, what is the surface area of the solid?

10. ABCD is a parallelogram (see figure). The ratio of DE to EC is 1 : 3. AE has a length of 3. If quadrilateral ABCE has an area of 21, what is the area of ABCD?

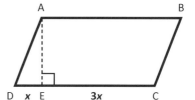

11. A swimming pool has a length of 30 meters, a width of 10 meters, and an average depth of 2 meters. If a hose can fill the pool at a rate of 0.5 cubic meters per minute, how many hours will it take the hose to fill the pool?

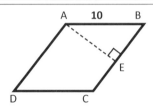

12.   ABCD is a rhombus (see figure). ABE is a right triangle.
      AB is 10 meters. The ratio of the length of CE to the length
      of EB is 2 to 3. What is the area of trapezoid AECD?

13.   A Rubix cube has an edge 5 inches long. What is the
      ratio of the cube's surface area to its volume?

14.   If the length of an edge of Cube A is one third the length of an edge of Cube B, what is
      the ratio of the volume of Cube A to the volume of Cube B?

15.   ABCD is a square picture frame (see figure). EFGH is a
      square inscribed within ABCD as a space for a picture. The
      area of EFGH (for the picture) is equal to the area of the
      picture frame (the area of ABCD minus the area of EFGH).
      If AB = 6, what is the length of EF?

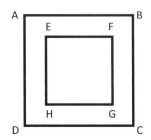

1. **54 feet:** We know that one side of the yard is 40 feet long; let us call this the length. We also know that the area of the yard is 280 square feet. In order to determine the perimeter, we must know the width of the yard.

$$A = l \times w$$
$$280 = 40w$$
$$w = 280 \div 40 = 7 \text{ feet}$$

Frank fences in the two 7-foot sides and one of the 40-foot sides. $40 + 2(7) = 54$.

2. **6 inches:** The perimeter of a pentagon is the sum of its five sides: $x + x + x + 3x + 3x = 9x$. If x is 2/3 of an inch, the perimeter is $9(2/3)$, or 6 inches.

3. **35 in²:** If E is the midpoint of C, then $CE = DE = x$. We can determine the length of x by using what we know about the area of triangle AED.

$$A = \frac{b \times h}{2} \qquad 12.5 = \frac{5x}{2}$$

$$25 = 5x$$
$$x = 5$$

Therefore, the length of CD is $2x$, or 10.

To find the area of the trapezoid, use the formula: $\quad A = \dfrac{b_1 + b_2}{2} \times h$

$$= \frac{4 + 10}{2} \times 5$$
$$= 35 \text{ in}^2$$

4. **$1,700:** To find the surface area of a rectangular solid, sum the individual areas of all six faces:

Top and Bottom:	$5 \times 4 = 20$	$\rightarrow$	$2 \times 20 = 40$
Side 1:	$5 \times 2.5 = 12.5$	$\rightarrow$	$2 \times 12.5 = 25$
Side 2:	$4 \times 2.5 = 10$	$\rightarrow$	$2 \times 10 = 20$

$$40 + 25 + 20 = 85 \text{ ft}^2$$

Covering the entire tank will cost $85 \times \$20 = \$1,700$.

5. **7:** The area of a triangle is equal to half the base times the height. Therefore, we can write the following relationship:

$$\frac{2y(y)}{2} = 49$$
$$y^2 = 49$$
$$y = 7$$

6. **90 ft²:** The area of the carpet is equal to $l \times w$, or 36 ft². Set up a percent table or a proportion to find the area of the whole living room floor:

$$\frac{40}{100} = \frac{36}{x}$$ Cross-multiply to solve.

$$40x = 3600$$
$$x = 90 \text{ ft}^2$$

7. **4:** Set up equations to represent the area and perimeter of the flower bed:

$$A = l \times w \hspace{4cm} P = 2(l + w)$$

Then, substitute the known values for the variables A and P:

$$44 = l \times w \hspace{4cm} 30 = 2(l + w)$$

Solve the two equations with the substitution method:

$$l = \frac{44}{w}$$

Multiply the entire equation by $\frac{w}{2}$.

$$30 = 2(\frac{44}{w} + w)$$

Solving the quadratic equation yields two solutions: 4 and 11. Since we are looking only for the length of the shorter side, the answer is 4.

$$15w = 44 + w^2$$
$$w^2 - 15w + 44 = 0$$
$$(w - 11)(w - 4) = 0$$
$$w = \{4, 11\}$$

Alternatively, you can arrive at the correct solution by picking numbers. What length and width add up to 15 (half of the perimeter) and multiply to produce 44 (the area)? Some experimentation will demonstrate that the longer side must be 11 and the shorter side must be 4.

8. $\dfrac{3}{x}$: If the length of the parking lot is $2x$ and the width is x, we can set up a fraction to represent the ratio of the perimeter to the area as follows:

$$\frac{\text{perimeter}}{\text{area}} = \frac{2(2x + x)}{(2x)(x)} = \frac{6x}{2x^2} = \frac{3}{x}$$

9. **144 m²:** The volume of a rectangular solid equals (length) × (width) × (height). If we know that the length and width are both 4 meters long, we can substitute values into the formulas as shown:

$$112 = 4 \times 4 \times h$$
$$h = 7$$

To find the surface area of a rectangular solid, sum the individual areas of all six faces:

Top and Bottom:	$4 \times 4 = 16$	$\rightarrow$	$2 \times 16 = 32$
Sides:	$4 \times 7 = 28$	$\rightarrow$	$4 \times 28 = 112$

$$32 + 112 = 144 \text{ m}^2$$

10. **24:** First, break quadrilateral ABCE into 2 pieces: a 3 by $3x$ rectangle and a right triangle with a base of x and a height of 3. Therefore, the area of quadrilateral ABCE is given by the following equation:

$$(3 \times 3x) + \frac{3 \times x}{2} = 9x + 1.5x = 10.5x$$

If ABCE has an area of 21, then $21 = 10.5x$, and $x = 2$. Quadrilateral ABCD is a parallelogram; thus, its area is equal to (base) × (height), or $4x \times 3$. Substitute the known value of 2 for x and simplify:

$$A = 4(2) \times 3 = 24$$

11. **20 hours:** The volume of the pool is (length) × (width) × (height), or $30 \times 10 \times 2 = 600$ cubic meters. Use a standard work equation, $RT = W$, where W represents the total work of 600 m³.

$$0.5t = 600$$
$$t = 1,200 \text{ minutes}$$
Convert this time to hours by dividing by 60: $1,200 \div 60 = 20$ hours.

12. **56 m²:** To find the area of a trapezoid, we need the lengths of both parallel bases and the height. If ABCD is a rhombus, then AD = AB = 10. This gives us the length of the first base, AD. We also know that CB = CE + EB = 10 and $\frac{CE}{EB} = \frac{2}{3}$. We can use the unknown multiplier method to find the length of the second base, CE:

$$2x + 3x = 10$$
$$5x = 10$$
$$x = 2$$
Thus, CE = $2x = 2(2) = 4$.

Now all that remains is the height of the trapezoid, AE. If you recognize that AE forms the long leg of a right triangle (ABE), you can use the Pythagorean Theorem to find the length of AE:
$$6^2 + b^2 = 10^2$$
$$b = 8$$

The area of the trapezoid is: $\dfrac{b_1 + b_2}{2} \times h = \dfrac{10 + 4}{2} \times 8 = 56 \text{ m}^2$.

13. $\dfrac{6}{5}$: To find the surface area of a cube, find the area of 1 face, and multiply that by 6: $6(5^2) = 150$. To find the volume of a cube, cube its edge length: $5^3 = 125$.

The ratio of the cube's surface area to its volume, therefore, is $\dfrac{150}{125}$, or $\dfrac{6}{5}$.

14. **1 to 27:** First, assign the variable x to the length of one side of Cube A. Then the length of one side of Cube B is $3x$. The volume of Cube A is x^3. The volume of Cube B is $(3x)^3$, or $27x^3$.

Therefore, the ratio of the volume of Cube A to Cube B is $\dfrac{x^3}{27x^3}$, or 1 to 27. You can also pick a number for the length of a side of Cube A and solve accordingly.

15. **$3\sqrt{2}$:** The area of the frame and the area of the picture sum to the total area of the image, which is 6^2, or 36. Therefore, the area of the frame and the picture are each equal to half of 36, or 18. Since EFGH is a square, the length of EF is $\sqrt{18}$, or $3\sqrt{2}$.

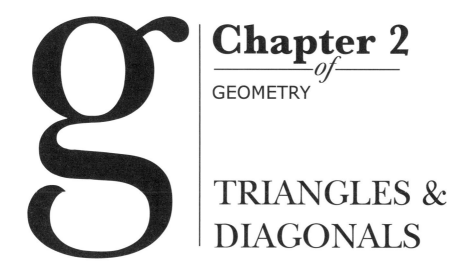

Chapter 2
of
GEOMETRY

TRIANGLES & DIAGONALS

In This Chapter . . .

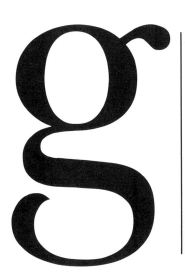

TRIANGLES & DIAGONALS

The polygon most commonly tested on the GMAT is the triangle.

Right triangles (those with a 90° angle) require particular attention, because they have special properties that are useful for solving many GMAT geometry problems.

The most important property of a right triangle is the unique relationship of the three sides. Given the lengths of any two of the sides of a right triangle, you can determine the length of the third side using the Pythagorean Theorem. There are even two special types of right triangles—the 30–60–90 triangle and the 45–45–90 triangle—for which you only need the length of ONE side to determine the lengths of the other two sides.

Finally, right triangles are essential for solving problems involving other polygons. For instance, you might cut more complex polygons into right triangles.

The sum of the interior angles of a triangle is 180°.

The Angles of a Triangle

The angles in any given triangle have two key properties:

(1) **The sum of the three angles of a triangle equals 180°.**

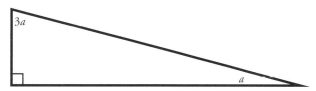

What is x? Since the sum of the three angles must be 180°, we can solve for x as follows:
$180 - 96 - 50 = x = 34°$.

What is a? Since the sum of the three angles must be 180°, we can solve for x as follows:
$90 + 3a + a = 180 \rightarrow a = 22.5°$.

(2) **Angles correspond to their opposite sides.** This means that the largest angle is opposite the longest side, while the smallest angle is opposite the shortest side. Additionally, **if two sides are equal, their opposite angles are also equal.** Such triangles are called **isosceles** triangles.

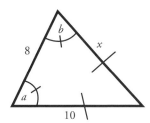

If angle a = angle b, what is the length of side x?

Since the side opposite angle b has a length of 10, the side opposite angle a must have the same length. Therefore, $x = 10$.

Mark equal angles and equal sides with a slash, as shown. Also be ready to redraw—often, a triangle that you know is isosceles is not displayed as such. To help your intuition, redraw the triangle to scale.

The Sides of a Triangle

Consider the following "impossible" triangle $\triangle ABC$ and what it reveals about the relationship between the three sides of any triangle.

The triangle to the right could never be drawn with the given measurements. Why? Consider that the shortest distance between any two points is a straight line. According to the triangle shown, the direct straight line distance between point C and point B is 14; however, the indirect path from point C to B (the path that goes from C to A to B) is 10 + 3, or 13, which is shorter than the direct path! This is clearly impossible.

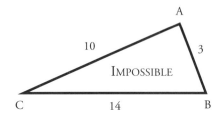

The above example leads to the following Triangle Inequality law:

The sum of any two sides of a triangle must be GREATER THAN the third side.

Therefore, the maximum integer distance for side BC in the triangle above is 12. If the length of side BC is not restricted to integers, then this length has to be **less than** 13.

Note that the length cannot be as small as we wish, either. It must be **greater than** the difference between the lengths of the other two sides. In this case, side BC must be longer than 10 − 3 = 7. This is a consequence of the same idea.

Consider the following triangle and the proof that the given measurements are possible:

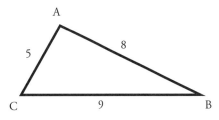

Test each combination of sides to prove that the measurements of this triangle are possible.

$$5 + 8 > 9$$
$$5 + 9 > 8$$
$$8 + 9 > 5$$

Note that the sum of two sides cannot be equal to the third side. The sum of two sides must always be **greater than** the third side.

If you are given two sides of a triangle, the length of the third side must lie between the difference and the sum of the two given sides. For instance, if you are told that two sides are of length 3 and 4, then the length of the third side must be between 1 and 7.

Margin note: The sum of any two sides of a triangle must be GREATER than the third side. This is called the Triangle Inequality Theorem.

The Pythagorean Theorem

A right triangle is a triangle with one right angle (90°). Every right triangle is composed of two **legs** and a **hypotenuse**. The hypotenuse is the side opposite the right angle and is often assigned the letter c. The two legs which form the right angle are often called a and b (it does not matter which leg is a and which leg is b).

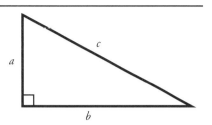

Given the lengths of two sides of a right triangle, how can you determine the length of the third side? Use the Pythagorean Theorem, which states that the sum of the square of the two legs of a right triangle ($a^2 + b^2$) is equal to the square of the hypotenuse of that triangle (c^2).

Pythagorean Theorem: $a^2 + b^2 = c^2$

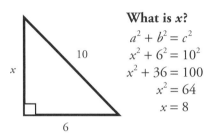

What is x?
$$a^2 + b^2 = c^2$$
$$x^2 + 6^2 = 10^2$$
$$x^2 + 36 = 100$$
$$x^2 = 64$$
$$x = 8$$

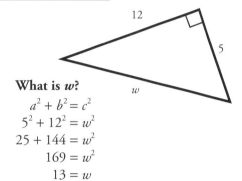

What is w?
$$a^2 + b^2 = c^2$$
$$5^2 + 12^2 = w^2$$
$$25 + 144 = w^2$$
$$169 = w^2$$
$$13 = w$$

Common Right Triangles

Certain right triangles appear over and over on the GMAT. It pays to memorize these common combinations in order to save time on the exam. Instead of using the Pythagorean Theorem to solve for the lengths of the sides of these common right triangles, you should know the following Pythagorean triples from memory:

Common Combinations	Key Multiples
3–4–5 The most popular of all right triangles $3^2 + 4^2 = 5^2$ ($9 + 16 = 25$)	6–8–10 9–12–15 12–16–20
5–12–13 Also quite popular on the GMAT $5^2 + 12^2 = 13^2$ ($25 + 144 = 169$)	10–24–26
8–15–17 This one appears less frequently $8^2 + 15^2 = 17^2$ ($64 + 225 = 289$)	None

Watch out for impostor triangles! A random triangle with one side equal to 3 and another side equal to 4 does not *necessarily* have a third side of length 5.

Whenever you see a right triangle on the GMAT, think about using the Pythagorean Theorem.

Manhattan **GMAT** Prep

Isosceles Triangles and the 45–45–90 Triangle

As previously noted, an isosceles triangle is one in which two sides are equal. The two angles opposite those two sides will also be equal. The most important isosceles triangle on the GMAT is the isosceles right triangle.

An isosceles right triangle has one 90° angle (opposite the hypotenuse) and two 45° angles (opposite the two equal legs). This triangle is called the 45–45–90 triangle.

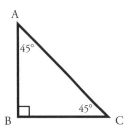

The lengths of the legs of every 45–45–90 triangle have a specific ratio, which you must memorize:

$$45° \rightarrow 45° \rightarrow 90°$$
leg	leg	hypotenuse
1 :	**1** :	$\sqrt{2}$
x :	x :	$x\sqrt{2}$

A 45–45–90 triangle is called an isosceles right triangle.

> Given that the length of side AB is 5, what are the lengths of sides BC and AC?

Since AB is 5, we use the ratio 1 : 1 : $\sqrt{2}$ for sides AB : BC : AC to determine that the multiplier x is 5. We then find that the sides of the triangle have lengths 5 : 5 : $5\sqrt{2}$. Therefore, the length of side BC = 5, and the length of side AC = $5\sqrt{2}$.

> Given that the length of side AC is $\sqrt{18}$, what are the lengths of sides AB and BC?

Since the hypotenuse AC is $\sqrt{18} = x\sqrt{2}$, we find that $x = \sqrt{18} \div \sqrt{2} = \sqrt{9} = 3$. Thus, the sides AB and BC are each equal to x, or 3.

One reason that the 45–45–90 triangle is so important is that this triangle is exactly half of a square! That is, two 45–45–90 triangles put together make up a square. Thus, if you are given the diagonal of a square, you can use the 45–45–90 ratio to find the length of a side of the square.

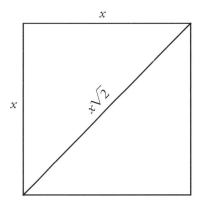

Equilateral Triangles and the 30–60–90 Triangle

An equilateral triangle is one in which all three sides (and all three angles) are equal. Each angle of an equilateral triangle is 60° (because all 3 angles must sum to 180°). A close relative of the equilateral triangle is the 30–60–90 triangle. Notice that two of these triangles, when put together, form an equilateral triangle:

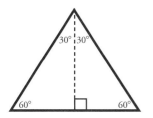

EQUILATERAL TRIANGLE

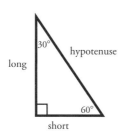

30–60–90 TRIANGLE

The lengths of the legs of every 30–60–90 triangle have the following ratio, which you must memorize:

30°	→	60°	→	90°
short leg		long leg		hypotenuse
1	:	$\sqrt{3}$	:	2
x	:	$x\sqrt{3}$	:	$2x$

Remember, $\sqrt{3}$ corresponds to the long leg of the triangle, and 2 corresponds to the hypotenuse, which is the longest side, because $\sqrt{3} < 2$.

> Given that the short leg of a 30–60–90 triangle has a length of 6, what are the lengths of the long leg and the hypotenuse?

The short leg, which is opposite the 30 degree angle, is 6. We use the ratio $1 : \sqrt{3} : 2$ to determine that the multiplier x is 6. We then find that the sides of the triangle have lengths 6: $6\sqrt{3}$: 12. The long leg measures $6\sqrt{3}$ and the hypotenuse measures 12.

> Given that an equilateral triangle has a side of length 10, what is its height?

Looking at the equilateral triangle above, we can see that the side of an equilateral triangle is the same as the hypotenuse of a 30–60–90 triangle. Additionally, the height of an equilateral triangle is the same as the long leg of a 30–60–90 triangle. Since we are told that the hypotenuse is 10, we use the ratio $x : x\sqrt{3} : 2x$ to set $2x = 10$ and determine that the multiplier x is 5. We then find that the sides of the 30–60–90 triangle have lengths 5 : $5\sqrt{3}$: 10. Thus, the long leg has a length of $5\sqrt{3}$, which is the height of the equilateral triangle.

If you get tangled up on a 30–60–90 triangle, try to find the length of the short leg. The other legs will then be easier to figure out.

Diagonals of Other Polygons

Right triangles are useful for more than just triangle problems. They are also helpful for finding the diagonals of other polygons, specifically squares, cubes, rectangles, and rectangular solids.

The diagonal of a square can be found using this formula:
$d = s\sqrt{2}$, where s is a side of the square.
This is also the face diagonal of a cube.

The main diagonal of a cube can be found using this formula:
$d = s\sqrt{3}$, where s is an edge of the cube.

Given a square with a side of length 5, what is the length of the diagonal of the square?

Using the formula $d = s\sqrt{2}$, we find that the length of the diagonal of the square is $5\sqrt{2}$.

What is the measure of an edge of a cube with a main diagonal of length $\sqrt{60}$?

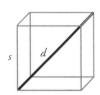

Again, using the formula $d = s\sqrt{3}$, we solve as follows:

$$\sqrt{60} = s\sqrt{3} \rightarrow s = \frac{\sqrt{60}}{\sqrt{3}} = \sqrt{20}$$

Thus, the length of the edge of the cube is $\sqrt{20}$.

Recall that the diagonal of a square is the hypotenuse of a 45–45–90 triangle.

To find the diagonal of a rectangle, you must know EITHER the length and the width OR one dimension and the proportion of one to the other.

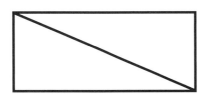

If the rectangle to the left has a length of 12 and a width of 5, what is the length of the diagonal?

Using the Pythagorean Theorem, we solve:
$$5^2 + 12^2 = c^2 \rightarrow 25 + 144 = c^2 \rightarrow c = 13$$

The diagonal length is 13.

If the rectangle above has a width of 6, and the ratio of the width to the length is 3 : 4, what is the diagonal?

Using the ratio, we find that the length is 8. Then we can use the Pythagorean Theorem. Alternatively, we can recognize that this is a 6–8–10 triangle. Either way, we find that the diagonal length is 10.

What is the length of the main diagonal of this rectangular solid?

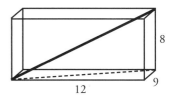

To find the diagonal of a rectangular solid, you can use the Pythagorean Theorem twice.

First, find the diagonal of the bottom face: $9^2 + 12^2 = c^2$ yields $c = 15$ (this is a multiple of a 3–4–5 triangle), so the bottom (dashed) diagonal is 15. Then, we can consider this bottom diagonal of length 15 as the base leg of another right triangle with a height of 8. Now we use the Pythagorean Theorem a second time: $8^2 + 15^2 = c^2$ yields $c = 17$, so the main diagonal is 17.

Generalizing this approach, we find the "Deluxe" Pythagorean Theorem: $d^2 = x^2 + y^2 + z^2$, where x, y, and z are the sides of the rectangular solid and d is the main diagonal. In this case, we could also solve this problem by applying the equation $9^2 + 12^2 + 8^2 = d^2$, yielding $d = 17$.

Similar Triangles

One final tool that you can use for GMAT triangle problems is the similar triangle strategy. Often, looking for similar triangles can help you solve complex problems.

Triangles are defined as similar if all their corresponding angles are **equal** and their **corresponding sides are in proportion**.

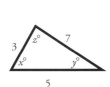
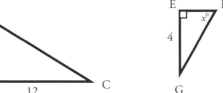

Once you find that 2 triangles have 2 pairs of equal angles, you know that the triangles are similar. If 2 sets of angles are congruent, then the third set of angles must be congruent, since the sum of the angles in any triangle is 180°.

What is the length of side EF?

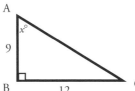

If two right triangles
have one other angle
in common, they are
similar triangles.

We know that the two triangles above are similar, because they have 2 angles in common (*x* and the right angle). Since they are similar triangles, their corresponding sides must be in proportion.

Side BC corresponds to side EG (since they both are opposite angle *x*). Since these sides are in the ratio of 12 : 4, we can determine that the large triangle is three times bigger than the smaller one. That is, the triangles are in the ratio of 3 : 1. Since side AB corresponds to side EF, and AB has a length of 9, we can conclude that side EF has a length of 3.

If we go on to compute the areas of these two triangles, we get the following results:

$$\text{Area of ABC} = \frac{1}{2}bh \qquad \text{Area of EFG} = \frac{1}{2}bh$$
$$= \frac{1}{2}(9)(12) \qquad\qquad = \frac{1}{2}(3)(4)$$
$$= 54 \qquad\qquad\qquad = 6$$

These two areas are in the ratio of 54 : 6, or 9 : 1. Notice the connection between this 9:1 ratio of areas and the 3 : 1 ratio of side lengths. The 9 : 1 ratio is simply the 3:1 ratio <u>squared</u>.

This observation can be generalized:

> **If two similar triangles have corresponding side lengths in ratio a:b, then their areas will be in ratio $a^2 : b^2$.**

The lengths being compared do not have to be sides—they can represent heights or perimeters. In fact, the figures do not have to be triangles. The principle holds true for *any* similar figures: quadrilaterals, pentagons, etc. For similar solids with corresponding sides in ratio $a : b$, their volumes will be in ratio $a^3 : b^3$.

Triangles and Area, Revisited

Although you may commonly think of "the base" of a triangle as whichever side is drawn horizontally, you can designate any side of a triangle as the base. For example, the following three diagrams show the same triangle, with each side in turn designated as the base:

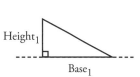 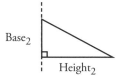 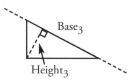

Since a triangle only has one area, the area must be the same regardless of the side chosen as the base. In other words,

$$\frac{1}{2} \times Base_1 \times Height_1 = \frac{1}{2} \times Base_2 \times Height_2 = \frac{1}{2} \times Base_3 \times Height_3$$

and therefore

$$Base_1 \times Height_1 = Base_2 \times Height_2 = Base_3 \times Height_3$$

Be able to see any side of a triangle as the base, not just the side that happens to be drawn horizontally. Also be able to draw the height from that base.

Right triangles have three possible bases just as other triangles do, but they are special because their two legs are perpendicular. Therefore, if one of the legs is chosen as the base, then the other leg is the height. Of course, we can also choose the hypotenuse as the base.

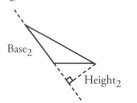 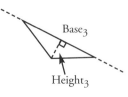

Thus, the area of a right triangle is given by the following formulas:

$$A = \frac{1}{2} \times (One\ leg) \times (Other\ leg) = \frac{1}{2} \times Hypotenuse \times Height\ from\ hypotenuse$$

Because an **equilateral triangle** can be split into two 30–60–90 triangles, a useful formula can be derived for its area. If the side length of the equilateral triangle is S, then S is also the hypotenuse of each of the 30–60–90 triangles, so their sides are as shown in the diagram.

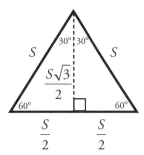

The equilateral triangle has base of length S and a height of length $\frac{S\sqrt{3}}{2}$. Therefore, the **area of an equilateral triangle with a side of length S is equal to** $\frac{1}{2}(S)\left(\frac{S\sqrt{3}}{2}\right) = \frac{S^2\sqrt{3}}{4}$.

Knowing this formula can save you significant time on a problem involving the area of an equilateral triangle, although you can always solve for the area without this formula.

Problem Set (Note: Figures are not drawn to scale.)

1. A square is bisected into two equal triangles (see figure). If the length of BD is $16\sqrt{2}$ inches, what is the area of the square?

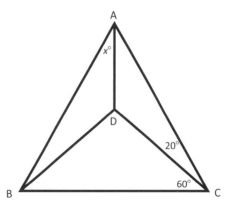

2. Beginning in Town A, Biker Bob rides his bike 10 miles west, 3 miles north, 5 miles east, and then 9 miles north, to Town B. How far apart are Town A and Town B? (Ignore the curvature of the earth.)

3. Now in Town B, Biker Bob walks due west, and then straight north to Town C. If Town B and Town C are 26 miles apart, and Biker Bob went 10 miles west, how many miles north did he go? (Again, ignore the curvature of the earth.)

4. Triangle A has a base of x and a height of $2x$. Triangle B is similar to Triangle A, and has a base of $2x$. What is the ratio of the area of Triangle A to Triangle B?

5. What is the measure of angle x in the figure to the right?

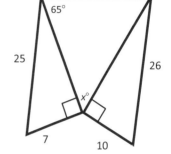

6. The longest side of an isosceles right triangle measures $20\sqrt{2}$. What is the area of the triangle?

7. Two similar triangles have areas in the ratio of 9 : 1. What is the ratio of these triangles' perimeters?

8. The size of a square computer screen is measured by the length of its diagonal. How much bigger is the visible area of a square 24-inch screen than the area of a square 20-inch screen?

9. A square field has an area of 400 square meters. Posts are set at all corners of the field. What is the longest distance between any two posts?

10. In Triangle ABC, AD = DB = DC (see figure). Given that angle DCB is 60° and angle ACD is 20°, what is the measure of angle x?

11. Two sides of a triangle are 4 and 10. If the third side is an integer x, how many possible values are there for x?

12. Jack makes himself a clay box in the shape of a cube, the edges of which are 4 inches long. What is the longest object he could fit inside the box (i.e., what is the diagonal of the cube)?

13.   What is the area of an equilateral triangle whose sides measure 8 cm long?

14.   Alexandra wants to pack away her posters without bending them. She rolls up the posters to put in a rectangular box that is 120 inches long, 90 inches wide, and 80 inches high. What is the longest a poster can be for Alexandra to pack it away without bending it (i.e., what is the diagonal of the rectangular box)?

15.   The points of a six-pointed star consist of six identical equilateral triangles, with each side 4 cm (see figure). What is the area of the entire star, including the center?

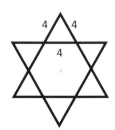

1. **256 square units:** The diagonal of a square is $s\sqrt{2}$; therefore, the side length of square ABCD is 16. The area of the square is s^2, or $16^2 = 256$.

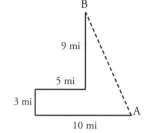

2. **13 miles:** If you draw a rough sketch of the path Biker Bob takes, as shown to the right, you can see that the direct distance from A to B forms the hypotenuse of a right triangle. The short leg (horizontal) is $10 - 5 = 5$ miles, and the long leg (vertical) is $9 + 3 = 12$ miles. Therefore, you can use the Pythagorean Theorem to find the direct distance from A to B:

$$5^2 + 12^2 = c^2$$
$$25 + 144 = c^2$$
$$c^2 = 169 \qquad \text{You might recognize the common right triangle:}$$
$$c = 13 \qquad \text{5–12–13.}$$

3. **24 miles:** If you draw a rough sketch of the path Biker Bob takes, as shown to the right, you can see that the direct distance from B to C forms the hypotenuse of a right triangle.

$$10^2 + b^2 = 26^2 \qquad \text{To find the square root of 576, you may find}$$
$$100 + b^2 = 676 \qquad \text{it helpful to prime factor it first:}$$
$$b^2 = 576 \qquad 576 = 2^6 \times 3^2$$
$$b = 24 \qquad \text{Therefore, } \sqrt{576} = 2^3 \times 3 = 24.$$

You might recognize this as a multiple of the common 5–12–13 triangle.

4. **1 to 4:** Since we know that Triangle B is similar to Triangle A, we can set up a proportion to represent the relationship between the sides of both triangles:

$$\frac{\text{base}}{\text{height}} = \frac{x}{2x} = \frac{2x}{?}$$

By proportional reasoning, the height of Triangle B must be $4x$. Calculate the area of each triangle with the formula:

Triangle A: $\qquad A = \dfrac{b \times h}{2} = \dfrac{(x)(2x)}{2} = x^2$

Triangle B: $\qquad A = \dfrac{b \times h}{2} = \dfrac{(2x)(4x)}{2} = 4x^2$

The ratio of the area of Triangle A to Triangle B is 1 to 4. Alternatively, we can simplify square the base ratio of 1 : 2.

5. **50°:** Use the Pythagorean Theorem to establish the missing lengths of the two right triangles on the right and left sides of the figure:

$$7^2 + b^2 = 25^2 \qquad\qquad 10^2 + b^2 = 26^2$$
$$49 + b^2 = 625 \qquad\qquad 100 + b^2 = 676$$
$$b^2 = 576 \qquad\qquad\quad b^2 = 576$$
$$b = 24 \qquad\qquad\qquad b = 24$$

The inner triangle is isosceles. Therefore, both angles opposite the equal sides measure 65°. Since there are 180° in a right triangle, $x = 180 - 2(65) = 50°$.

Manhattan **GMAT** Prep
the new standard

6. **200:** An isosceles right triangle is a 45–45–90 triangle, with sides in the ratio of $1 : 1 : \sqrt{2}$. If the longest side, the hypotenuse, measures $20\sqrt{2}$, the two other sides each measure 20. Therefore, the area of the triangle is:

$$A = \frac{b \times h}{2} = \frac{20 \times 20}{2} = 200$$

7. **3 to 1:** If two triangles have areas in the ratio of 9 to 1, then their linear measurements have a ratio of $\sqrt{9}$ to $\sqrt{1}$, or 3 to 1. You can derive this rule algebraically with the following reasoning:

Imagine two similar triangles: a smaller one with base b and height h, and a larger one with base bx and height hx. The ratio of the areas of the larger triangle to the smaller one, therefore, would be:

$$\frac{0.5(bx \times hx)}{0.5(b \times h)} = \frac{0.5bhx^2}{0.5bh} = \frac{x^2}{1}$$ If we know that $x^2 = 9$, then $x = 3$. The ratio of the linear measurements (perimeter) is 3 to 1.

We can also simply square-root the area ratio of $9 : 1$ and get the length ratio of $3 : 1$.

Alternately, solve this problem by picking real numbers. To do so, create two triangles whose areas have a 9:1 ratio.

First, draw the smaller triangle with an area of 6. Since the area of a triangle is half the product of the base and the height, the base and the height must multiply to 12. If possible, use a common right triangle: $3 \times 4 = 12$.

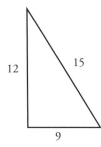

$$A_{\text{small}} = \frac{bh}{2} = \frac{3 \times 4}{2} = 6$$

Now draw the larger triangle. Since the smaller triangle has an area of 6, we need to draw a larger triangle with an area 9 times larger. $6 \times 9 = 54$. Since the area of a triangle is half the product of the base and height, the base and height must multiply to 108. Thus, we will use a right triangle with sides of length 9 and 12: $9 \times 12 = 108$.

$$A_{\text{large}} = \frac{bh}{2} = \frac{9 \times 12}{2} = 54$$

Then find the ratio of the perimeters: $\dfrac{9 + 12 + 15}{3 + 4 + 5} = \dfrac{36}{12} = 3$.

8. **88 in²:** If the diagonal of the larger screen is 24 inches, and we know that $d = s\sqrt{2}$, then:

$$s = \frac{d}{\sqrt{2}} = \frac{24}{\sqrt{2}} = 12\sqrt{2}.$$

By the same reasoning, the side length of the smaller screen is $\dfrac{20}{\sqrt{2}} = 10\sqrt{2}$.

The areas of the two screens are:

Large screen: $A = 12\sqrt{2} \times 12\sqrt{2} = 288$

Small screen: $A = 10\sqrt{2} \times 10\sqrt{2} = 200$

The visible area of the larger screen is 88 square inches bigger than the visible area of the smaller screen.

Manhattan GMAT® Prep
the new standard

9: **20√2:** The longest distance between any two posts is the diagonal of the field. If the area of the field is 400 square meters, then each side must measure 20 meters. Diagonal = $d = s\sqrt{2}$, so $d = 20\sqrt{2}$.

10. **10:** If AD = DB = DC, then the three triangular regions in this figure are all isosceles triangles. Therefore, we can fill in some of the missing angle measurements as shown to the right. Since we know that there are 180° in the large triangle ABC, we can write the following equation:

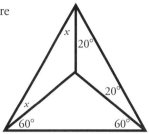

$$x + x + 20 + 20 + 60 + 60 = 180$$
$$2x + 160 = 180$$
$$x = 10$$

11. **7:** If two sides of a triangle are 4 and 10, the third side must be greater than $10 - 4$ and smaller than $10 + 4$. Therefore, the possible values for x are {7, 8, 9, 10, 11, 12, and 13}. You can draw a sketch to convince yourself of this result:

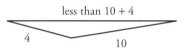

12. **4√3:** The diagonal of a cube with side s is $s\sqrt{3}$. Therefore, the longest object Jack could fit inside the box would be $4\sqrt{3}$ inches long.

13. **16√3:** Draw in the height of the triangle (see figure). If triangle ABC is an equilateral triangle, and ABD is a right triangle, then ABD is a 30–60–90 triangle. Therefore, its sides are in the ratio of $1 : \sqrt{3} : 2$. If the hypotenuse is 8, the short leg is 4, and the long leg is $4\sqrt{3}$. This is the height of triangle ABC. Find the area of triangle ABC with the formula for area of a triangle:

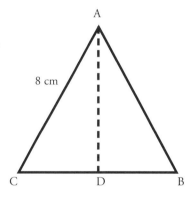

$$A = \frac{b \times h}{2} = \frac{8 \times 4\sqrt{3}}{2} = 16\sqrt{3}$$

Alternatively, you can apply the formula $A = \dfrac{S^2\sqrt{3}}{4}$, yielding $A = \dfrac{8^2\sqrt{3}}{4} = \dfrac{64\sqrt{3}}{4} = 16\sqrt{3}$.

14. **170 inches:** Find the diagonal of this rectangular solid by applying the Pythagorean Theorem twice. First, find the diagonal across the bottom of the box:

$$120^2 + 90^2 = c^2$$
$$14{,}400 + 8100 = c^2$$
$$c^2 = 22{,}500$$
$$c = 150$$

You might recognize this as a multiple of the common 3–4–5 right triangle.

Then, find the diagonal of the rectangular box:

$$80^2 + 150^2 = c^2$$
$$6400 + 22{,}500 = c^2$$
$$c^2 = 28{,}900$$
$$c = 170$$

You might recognize this as a multiple of the common 8–15–17 right triangle.

15. **$48\sqrt{3}$ cm²:** We can think of this star as a large equilateral triangle with sides 12 cm long, and three additional smaller equilateral triangles with sides 4 inches long. Using the same 30–60–90 logic we applied in problem #13, we can see that the height of the larger equilateral triangle is $6\sqrt{3}$, and the height of the smaller equilateral triangle is $2\sqrt{3}$. Therefore, the areas of the triangles are as follows:

Large triangle: $A = \dfrac{b \times h}{2} = \dfrac{12 \times 6\sqrt{3}}{2} = 36\sqrt{3}$

Small triangles: $A = \dfrac{b \times h}{2} = \dfrac{4 \times 2\sqrt{3}}{2} = 4\sqrt{3}$

The total area of three smaller triangles and one large triangle is:
$$36\sqrt{3} + 3(4\sqrt{3}) = 48\sqrt{3} \text{ cm}^2.$$

Alternatively, you can apply the formula $A = \dfrac{S^2\sqrt{3}}{4}$.

Large triangle: $A = \dfrac{12^2\sqrt{3}}{4} = \dfrac{144\sqrt{3}}{4} = 36\sqrt{3}.$

Small triangle: $A = \dfrac{4^2\sqrt{3}}{4} = \dfrac{16\sqrt{3}}{4} = 4\sqrt{3}.$

Then add the area of the large triangle and the area of three smaller triangles, as above.

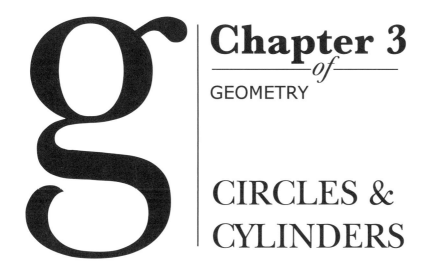

Chapter 3
of

GEOMETRY

CIRCLES & CYLINDERS

In This Chapter . . .

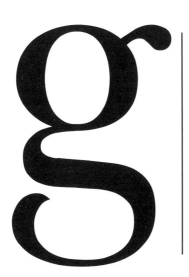

CIRCLES & CYLINDERS

A circle is defined as the set of points in a plane that are equidistant from a fixed center point. A circle contains 360° (360 degrees).

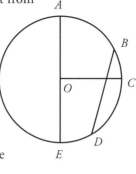

Any line segment that connects the center point to a point on the circle is termed a **radius** of the circle. If point O is the center of the circle shown to the right, then segment OC is a radius.

Any line segment that connects two points on a circle is called a **chord**. Any chord that passes through the center of the circle is called a **diameter**. Notice that the diameter is two times the length of the radius. Line segment BD is a chord of the circle shown to the right. Line segment AE is a diameter of the circle.

The GMAT tests your ability to find (1) the circumference and (2) the area of whole and partial circles. In addition, you must know how to work with cylinders, which are three-dimensional shapes made, in part, of circles. The GMAT tests your ability to find (3) the surface area and (4) the volume of cylinders.

If you know the circumference, the radius, the diameter, or the area of a circle, you can use one to find ANY of the other measurements.

Circumference of a Circle

The distance around a circle is termed the circumference. This is equivalent to the perimeter of a polygon. The only information you need to find the circumference of a circle is the radius of that circle. The formula for the circumference of any circle is:

$$C = 2\pi r$$

where C is the circumference, r is the radius, and π is a number that equals approximately 3.14.

For the purposes of the GMAT, π can usually be approximated as 3 (or as a number slightly larger than 3, such as 22/7). In fact, most problems require no approximation, since the GMAT includes π as part of the answer choices. For example, a typical answer choice for a circumference problem would be 8π, rather than 24.

> What is the distance around a circle that has a diameter of 10?

To solve this, first determine the radius, which is half of the diameter, or 5. Then plug this into the circumference formula $C = 2\pi r = 2\pi(5) = 10\pi$. (We could also note that the diameter of a circle equals twice the radius of the circle, so $d = 2r$. Therefore, $C = 2\pi r = \pi d$. In this case, the circumference equals 10π.)

The answer 10π is generally sufficient. You do not need to multiply 10 by π and get a decimal (31.4…) or a fraction. A precise decimal or fractional answer is in fact impossible. More importantly, knowing that π is approximately 3 can help you rule out unreasonably small or large answer choices if you are unable to get an exact answer.

Note also that a full revolution, or turn, of a spinning wheel is equivalent to the wheel going around once. A point on the edge of the wheel travels one circumference in one revolution. Note also that a full revolution, or turn, of a spinning wheel is equivalent to the wheel going around once. A point on the edge of the wheel travels one circumference in one revolution. For example, if a wheel spins at 3 revolutions per second, a point on the edge travels a distance equal to 3 circumferences per second. If the wheel has a diameter of 10 units, then the point travels at a rate of $3 \times 10\pi = 30\pi$ units per second.

Circumference and Arc Length

Often, the GMAT will ask you to solve for a portion of the distance on a circle, instead of the entire circumference. This portion is termed an **arc**. Arc length can be found by determining what fraction the arc is of the entire circumference. This can be done by looking at the central angle that defines the arc.

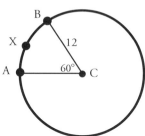

What is the length of arc AXB?

Arc AXB is the arc from A to B, passing through the point X. To find its length, first find the circumference of the circle. The radius is given as 12. To find the circumference, use the formula $C = 2\pi r = 2\pi(12) = 24\pi$.

There are a total of 360° in a circle.

Then, use the central angle to determine what fraction the arc is of the entire circle. Since the arc is defined by the central angle of 60 degrees, and the entire circle is 360 degrees,

then the arc is $\dfrac{60}{360} = \dfrac{1}{6}$ of the circle.

Therefore, the measure of arc AXB $= \left(\dfrac{1}{6}\right)(24\pi) = 4\pi$.

Perimeter of a Sector

The boundaries of a **sector** of a circle are formed by the arc and two radii. Think of a sector as a slice of pizza. The arc corresponds to the crust, and the center of the circle corresponds to the tip of the slice.

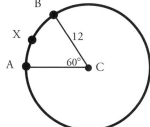

If you know the length of the radius and the central (or inscribed) angle, you can find the perimeter of the sector.

What is the perimeter of sector ABC?

In the previous example, we found the length of arc AXB to be 4π. Therefore, the perimeter of the sector is:

$$4\pi + 12 + 12 = 24 + 4\pi.$$

Area of a Circle

The space inside a circle is termed the area of the circle. This area is just like the area of a polygon. Just as with circumference, the only information you need to find the area of a circle is the radius of that circle. The formula for the area of any circle is:

$$A = \pi r^2$$

where A is the area, r is the radius, and π is a number that is approximately 3.14.

What is the area of a circle with a circumference of 16π?

In order to find the area of a circle, all we must know is its radius. If the circumference of the circle is 16π (and $C = 2\pi r$), then the radius must be 8. Plug this into the area formula:
$A = \pi r^2 = \pi(8^2) = 64\pi$.

Area of a Sector

Often, the GMAT will ask you to solve for the area of a sector of a circle, instead of the area of the entire circle. You can find the area of a sector by determining the fraction of the entire area that the sector occupies. To determine this fraction, look at the central angle that defines the sector.

What is the area of sector ACB (the striped region) below?

First, find the area of the entire circle:
$A = \pi r^2 = \pi(3^2) = 9\pi$.

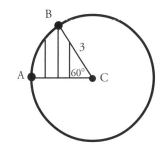

Then, use the central angle to determine what fraction of the entire circle is represented by the sector. Since the sector is defined by the central angle of $60°$, and the entire circle is $360°$, the sector occupies $60°/360°$, or one-sixth, of the area of the circle.

Therefore, the area of sector ACB is $\left(\dfrac{1}{6}\right)(9\pi) = 1.5\pi$.

Central or inscribed angles can help you determine arc length and sector area.

Inscribed vs. Central Angles

Thus far, in dealing with arcs and sectors, we have referred to the concept of a **central angle**. A central angle is defined as an angle whose vertex lies at the center point of a circle. As we have seen, a central angle defines both an arc and a sector of a circle.

Another type of angle is termed an **inscribed angle**. An inscribed angle has its vertex on the circle itself. The following diagrams illustrate the difference between a central angle and an inscribed angle.

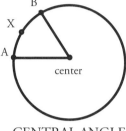 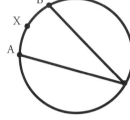 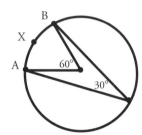

CENTRAL ANGLE   INSCRIBED ANGLE

Notice that, in the circle at the far right, there is a central angle and an inscribed angle, both of which intercept arc *AXB*. It is the central angle that defines the arc. That is, the arc is 60° (or one sixth of the complete 360° circle). **An inscribed angle is equal to half of the arc it intercepts**, in degrees. In this case, the inscribed angle is 30°, which is half of 60°.

Inscribed Triangles

Related to this idea of an inscribed angle is that of an **inscribed triangle**. A triangle is said to be inscribed in a circle if all of the vertices of the triangle are points on the circle. The important rule to remember is: **if one of the sides of an inscribed triangle is a DIAMETER of the circle, then the triangle MUST be a right triangle.** Conversely, any right triangle inscribed in a circle must have the diameter of the circle as one of its sides (thereby splitting the circle in half).

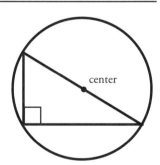

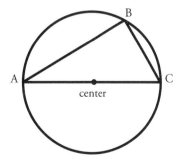

Above right is a special case of the rule mentioned above (that an inscribed angle is equal to half of the arc it intercepts, in degrees). In this case, the right angle (90°) lies opposite a semicircle, which is an arc that measures 180°.

In the inscribed triangle to the left, triangle ABC must be a right triangle, since AC is a diameter of the circle.

If you are given the measure of an inscribed angle, find the measure of the corresponding central angle to solve the problem.

Cylinders and Surface Area

Two circles and a rectangle combine to form a three-dimensional shape called a right circular cylinder (referred to from now on simply as a **cylinder**). The top and bottom of the cylinder are circles, while the middle of the cylinder is formed from a rolled-up rectangle, as shown in the diagram below:

In order to determine the surface area of a cylinder, sum the areas of the 3 surfaces: The area of each circle is πr^2, while the area of the rectangle is length × width. Looking at the figures on the left, we can see that the length of the rectangle is equal to the circumference of the circle ($2\pi r$), and the width of the rectangle is equal to the height of the cylinder (h). Therefore, the area of the rectangle is $2\pi r \times h$. To find the total surface area of a cylinder, add the area of the circular top and bottom, as well as the area of the rectangle that wraps around the outside.

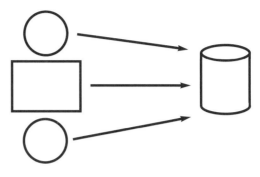

Think of the formula for the volume of a cylinder as the area of the circular base multiplied by the height, just like the formula for the volume of a rectangular solid.

$$SA = 2 \text{ circles} + \text{rectangle} = 2(\pi r^2) + 2\pi rh$$

The only information you need to find the surface area of a cylinder is (1) the radius of the cylinder and (2) the height of the cylinder.

Cylinders and Volume

The volume of a cylinder measures how much "stuff" it can hold inside. In order to find the volume of a cylinder, use the following formula.

$$V = \pi r^2 h$$

V is the volume, r is the radius of the cylinder, and h is the height of the cylinder.

As with finding surface area, determining the volume of a cylinder requires two pieces of information: (1) the radius of the cylinder and (2) the height of the cylinder.

The diagram below shows that two cylinders can have the same volume but different shapes (and therefore each fits differently inside a larger object).

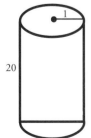

$$V = \pi r^2 h$$
$$= \pi(1)^2 20$$
$$= 20\pi$$

$$V = \pi r^2 h$$
$$= \pi(2)^2 5$$
$$= 20\pi$$

Problem Set (Note: Figures are not drawn to scale.)

1. Triangle ABC is inscribed in a circle, such that AC is a diameter of the circle (see figure). If AB has a length of 8 and BC has a length of 15, what is the circumference of the circle?

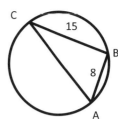

2. A cylinder has a surface area of 360π, and is 3 units tall. What is the diameter of the cylinder's circular base?

3. Randy can run π meters every 2 seconds. If the circular track has a radius of 75 meters, how long does it take Randy to run twice around the track?

4. Randy then moves on to the Jumbo Track, which has a radius of 200 meters (as compared to the first track, with a radius of 75 meters). Ordinarily, Randy runs 8 laps on the normal track. How many laps on the Jumbo Track would Randy have to run in order to have the same workout?

5. A circular lawn with a radius of 5 meters is surrounded by a circular walkway that is 4 meters wide (see figure). What is the area of the walkway?

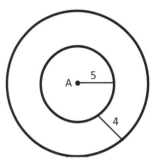

6. A cylindrical water tank has a diameter of 14 meters and a height of 20 meters. A water truck can fill π cubic meters of the tank every minute. How long will it take the water truck to fill the water tank from empty to half-full?

7. Red Giant cola comes in two sizes, Giant and Super-Giant. Each comes in a cylindrical container, and the Giant size sells for $1.20. If the Super-Giant container has twice the height and its circular base has twice the radius of the Giant size, and the price per ml of Red Giant cola is the same, how much does the Super-Giant container cost?

8. BE and CD are both diameters of Circle A (see figure). If the area of Circle A is 180 units^2, what is the area of sector ABC + sector ADE?

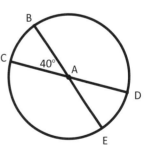

9. Jane has to paint a cylindrical column that is 14 feet high and that has a circular base with a radius of 3 feet. If one bucket of paint will cover 10π square feet, how many buckets does Jane need to buy in order to paint the column, including the top and bottom?

10. A rectangular box has the dimensions 12 inches × 10 inches × 8 inches. What is the largest possible volume of a right cylinder that is placed inside the box?

11. A circular flower bed takes up half the area of a square lawn. If an edge of the lawn is 200 feet long, what is the radius of the flower bed? (Express the answer in terms of π.)

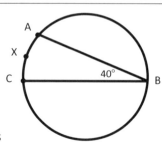

12.   If angle ABC is 40 degrees (see figure), and the area of the circle is 81π, how long is arc AXC?

13.   A Hydrogenator water gun has a cylindrical water tank, which is 30 centimeters long. Using a hose, Jack fills his Hydrogenator with π cubic centimeters of his water tank every second. If it takes him 8 minutes to fill the tank with water, what is the diameter of the circular base of the gun's water tank?

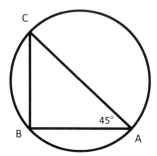

14.   Triangle ABC is inscribed in a circle, such that AC is a diameter of the circle and angle BAC is 45° (see figure). If the area of triangle ABC is 72 square units, how much larger is the area of the circle than the area of triangle ABC?

15.   Triangle ABC is inscribed in a circle, such that AC is a diameter of the circle and angle BAC is 45°. (Refer to the same figure as for problem #14.) If the area of triangle ABC is 84.5 square units, what is the length of arc BC?

1. **17π:** If AC is a diameter of the circle, then inscribed triangle ABC is a right triangle, with AC as the hypotenuse. Therefore, we can apply the Pythagorean Theorem to find the length of AC.

$$8^2 + 15^2 = c^2$$
$$64 + 225 = c^2 \qquad\qquad \text{The circumference of the circle is } 2\pi r, \text{ or } 17\pi.$$
$$c^2 = 289$$
$$c = 17 \qquad\qquad \text{You might recognize the common 8–15–17 right triangle.}$$

2. **24:** The surface area of a cylinder is the area of the circular top and bottom, plus the area of its wrapped-around rectangular third face. We can express this in formula form as:

$$SA = 2(\pi r^2) + 2\pi rh$$

Substitute the known values into this formula to find the radius of the circular base:

$$360\pi = 2(\pi r^2) + 2\pi r(3)$$
$$360\pi = 2\pi r^2 + 6\pi r$$
$$r^2 + 3r - 180 = 0$$
$$(r + 15)(r - 12) = 0$$

$$r + 15 = 0 \qquad \text{OR} \qquad r - 12 = 0$$
$$r = \{-15, 12\}$$

Use only the positive value of r: 12. If $r = 12$, the diameter of the cylinder's circular base is 24.

3. **10 minutes:** The distance around the track is the circumference of the circle:

$$C = 2\pi r$$
$$= 150\pi$$

Running twice around the circle would equal a distance of 300π meters. If Randy can run π meters every 2 seconds, he runs 30π meters every minute. Therefore, it will take him 10 minutes to run around the circular track twice.

4. **3 laps:** 8 laps on the normal track is a distance of $1{,}200\pi$ meters. (Recall from problem #3 that the circumference of the normal track is 150π meters.) If the Jumbo Track has a radius of 200 meters, its circumference is 400π meters. It will take 3 laps around this track to travel $1{,}200\pi$ meters.

5. **$56\pi m^2$:** The area of the walkway is the area of the entire image (walkway + lawn) minus the area of the lawn. To find the area of each circle, use the formula:

Large circle: $A = \pi r^2 = \pi(9)^2 = 81\pi$
Small circle: $A = \pi r^2 = \pi(5)^2 = 25\pi$ $81\pi - 25\pi = 56\pi m^2$

6. **8 hours and 10 minutes:** First find the volume of the cylindrical tank:

$$V = \pi r^2 \times h$$
$$= \pi(7)^2 \times 20$$
$$= 980\pi$$

If the water truck can fill π cubic meters of the tank every minute, it will take 980 minutes to fill the tank completely; therefore, it will take $980 \div 2 = 490$ minutes to fill the tank halfway. This is equal to 8 hours and 10 minutes.

7. **$9.60:** Let h = the height of the giant size → $2h$ = the height of the super-giant size.
         Let r = the radius of the giant size → $2r$ = the radius of the super-giant size.

The volume of the giant can = $\pi r^2 h$.
The volume of the super-giant can = $\pi(2r)^2 \times 2h = 8(\pi r^2 \times h) = 8\pi r^2 h$.
The super-giant can holds 8 times as much cola. If the price per ml is the same, and the Giant can sells for $1.20, the Super-Giant can sells for 8($1.20) = $9.60.

8. **40 units²:** The two central angles, CAB and DAE, describe a total of 80°. Simplify the fraction to find out what fraction of the circle this represents:

$$\frac{80}{360} = \frac{2}{9} \qquad\qquad \frac{2}{9} \text{ of } 180 \text{ units}^2 \text{ is } 40 \text{ units}^2.$$

9. **11 buckets:** The surface area of a cylinder is the area of the circular top and bottom, plus the area of its wrapped-around rectangular third face.

     Top & Bottom: $A = \pi r^2 = 9\pi$
     Rectangle: $A = 2\pi r \times h = 84\pi$

The total surface area, then, is $9\pi + 9\pi + 84\pi = 102\pi$ ft². If one bucket of paint will cover 10π ft², then Jane will need 10.2 buckets to paint the entire column. Since paint stores do not sell fractional buckets, she will need to purchase 11 buckets.

10. **200π:** The radius of the cylinder must be equal to half of the smaller of the 2 dimensions that form the box's bottom. The height, then, can be equal to the remaining dimension of the box.

There is no general way to tell which way the cylinder will have the largest dimension; you must simply try all possibilities:

$V = \pi r^2 \times h$
Case 1: $r = 5$, $h = 8$ Case 2: $r = 4$, $h = 10$ Case 3: $r = 4$, $h = 12$
$V = 25\pi \times 8 = 200\pi$ $V = 16\pi \times 10 = 160\pi$ $V = 16\pi \times 12 = 192\pi$

Case 1 yields the largest volume. (Case 2 can be seen to be inferior right away, because it makes no use of the largest dimension of the box.)

11. $\sqrt{\dfrac{20,000}{\pi}}$ **:** The area of the lawn is $(200)^2 = 40,000$ ft².

Therefore, the area of the flower bed is $40,000 \div 2 = 20,000$ ft².

$A = \pi r^2 = 20,000$ The radius of the flower bed is equal to $\sqrt{\dfrac{20,000}{\pi}}$.

12. **4π:** If the area of the circle is 81π, then the radius of the circle is 9 ($A = \pi r^2$). Therefore, the total circumference of the circle is 18π ($C = 2\pi r$). Angle ABC, an inscribed angle of 40°, corresponds to a central angle of 80°. Thus, arc *AXC* is equal to 80/360 = 2/9 of the total circumference:

     $2/9(18\pi) = 4\pi$.

13. **8 cm:** In 8 minutes, or 480 seconds, 480 πcm^3 of water flows into the tank. Therefore, the volume of the tank is 480π. We are given a height of 30, so we can solve for the radius.

$$V = \pi r^2 \times h$$
$$480\pi = 30\pi r^2$$
$$r^2 = 16$$
$$r = 4$$

Therefore, the diameter of the tank's base is 8 cm.

14. **72π − 72:** If AC is a diameter of the circle, then angle ABC is a right angle. Therefore, triangle ABC is a 45–45–90 triangle, and the base and height are equal. Assign the variable x to represent both the base and height:

$$A = \frac{bh}{2} \qquad\qquad \frac{x^2}{2} = 72$$
$$x^2 = 144$$
$$x = 12$$

The base and height of the triangle are equal to 12, and so the area of the triangle is $\frac{12 \times 12}{2} = 72$.

The hypotenuse of the triangle, which is also the diameter of the circle, is equal to $12\sqrt{2}$. Therefore, the radius is equal to $6\sqrt{2}$ and the area of the circle, πr^2, $= 72\pi$. The area of the circle is $72\pi − 72$ square units larger than the area of triangle ABC.

15. $\dfrac{13\sqrt{2}\pi}{4}$: We know that the area of triangle ABC is 84.5 square units, so we can use the same logic as in the previous problem to establish the base and height of the triangle:

$$A = \frac{bh}{2} \qquad\qquad \frac{x^2}{2} = 84.5$$
$$x^2 = 169$$
$$x = 13$$

The base and height of the triangle are equal to 13. Therefore, the hypotenuse, which is also the diameter of the circle, is equal to $13\sqrt{2}$, and the circumference ($C = \pi d$) is equal to $13\sqrt{2}\pi$. Angle A, an inscribed angle, corresponds to a central angle of 90°. Thus, arc BC = 90/360 = 1/4 of the total circumference:

$$\frac{1}{4} \text{ of } 13\sqrt{2}\pi \text{ is } \frac{13\sqrt{2}\pi}{4}.$$

g

Chapter 4
of

GEOMETRY

LINES &
ANGLES

In This Chapter . . .

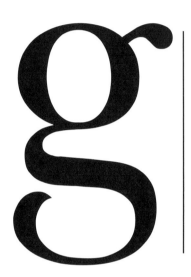

- Intersecting Lines
- Exterior Angles of a Triangle
- Parallel Lines Cut by a Transversal

LINES & ANGLES

A straight line is the shortest distance between 2 points. As an angle, a line measures 180°.

Parallel lines are lines that lie in a plane and that never intersect. No matter how far you extend the lines, they never meet. Two parallel lines are shown below:

Perpendicular lines are lines that intersect at a 90° angle. Two perpendicular lines are shown below:

There are two major line-angle relationships that you must know for the GMAT:
    (1) The angles formed by any intersecting lines.
    (2) The angles formed by parallel lines cut by a transversal.

> There are 180° in a straight line.

Intersecting Lines

Intersecting lines have three important properties.

First, the interior angles formed by intersecting lines form a circle, so the sum of these angles is 360°. In the diagram shown, $a + b + c + d = 360$.

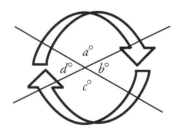

Second, interior angles that combine to form a line sum to 180°. These are termed **supplementary angles**. Thus, in the diagram shown, $a + b = 180$, because angles a and b form a line together. Other supplementary angles are $b + c = 180$, $c + d = 180$, and $d + a = 180$.

Third, angles found opposite each other where these two lines intersect are equal. These are called **vertical angles**. Thus, in the diagram above, $a = c$, because both of these angles are opposite each other, and are formed from the same two lines. Additionally, $b = d$ for the same reason.

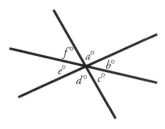

Note that these rules apply to more than two lines that intersect at a point, as shown to the left. In this diagram, $a + b + c + d + e + f = 360$, because these angles combine to form a circle. In addition, $a + b + c = 180$, because these three angles combine to form a line. Finally, $a = d$, $b = e$, and $c = f$, because they are pairs of vertical angles.

*Manhattan*GMAT*Prep
the new standard

Exterior Angles of a Triangle

An **exterior angle** of a triangle is equal in measure to the sum of the two non-adjacent (opposite) **interior angles** of the triangle. For example:

$a + b + c = 180$ (sum of angles in a triangle).
$b + x = 180$ (supplementary angles).
Therefore, $x = a + c$.

Sometimes parallel lines cut by a transversal appear when a rectangle, a parallel-ogram, a rhombus, or a trapezoid is cut in half by a diagonal.

This property is frequently tested on the GMAT! In particular, look for exterior angles within more complicated diagrams. You might even redraw the diagram with certain lines removed to isolate the triangle and exterior angle you need.

Parallel Lines Cut By a Transversal

The GMAT makes frequent use of diagrams that include parallel lines cut by a **transversal**.

Notice that there are 8 angles formed by this con-struction, but there are only TWO different angle measures (a and b). All the **acute** angles (less than 90°) in this diagram are equal. Likewise, all the **obtuse** angles (more than 90° but less than 180°) are equal. Any acute angle is supplementary to any obtuse angle. Thus, $a + b = 180°$.

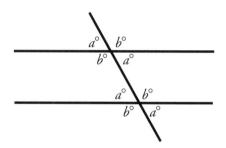

When you see a transversal cutting two lines that you know to be parallel, fill in all the a (acute) and b (obtuse) angles, just as in the diagram above.

Sometimes the GMAT disguises the parallel lines and the transversal so that they are not readily apparent, as in the diagram pictured to the right. In these disguised cases, it is a good idea to extend the lines so that you can easily see the parallel lines and the transversal. Just remember always to be on the lookout for parallel lines. When you see them, extend lines and label the acute and obtuse angles. You might also mark the parallel lines with arrows, as shown below to the right.

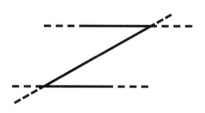

The GMAT uses the symbol || to indicate in text that two lines or line segments are parallel. For instance, if you see $\overline{MN} \,\|\, \overline{OP}$ in a problem, you know that line segment $\overline{MN}$ is parallel to line segment $\overline{OP}$.

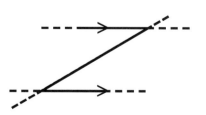

*Manhattan*GMAT*Prep
the new standard

Problem Set

Problems 1–4 refer to the diagram below, where line AB is parallel to line CD.

1.   If $x - y = 10$, what is x?

2.   If the ratio of x to y is 3 : 2, what is y?

3.   If $x + (x + y) = 320$, what is x?

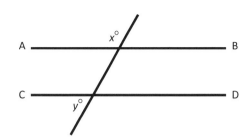

4.   If $\dfrac{x}{x - y} = 2$, what is x?

Problems 5–8 refer to the diagram below.

5.   If a is 95, what is $b + d - e$?

6.   If $c + f = 70$, and $d = 80$, what is b?

7.   If a and b are **complementary angles** (they sum to 90°), name three other pairs of complementary angles.

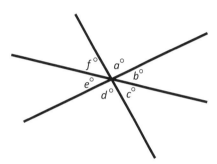

8.   If e is 45, what is the sum of all the other angles?

Problems 9–12 refer to the diagram below, where line XY is parallel to line QU.

9.   If $a + e = 150$, find f.

10.   If $a = y$, $g = 3y + 20$, and $f = 2x$, find x.

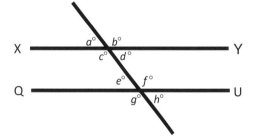

11.   If $g = 11y$, $a = 4x - y$, and $d = 5y + 2x - 20$, find h.

12.   If $b = 4x$, $e = x + 2y$, and $d = 3y + 8$, find h.

Problems 13–15 refer to the diagram to the right.

13.   If $c + g = 140$, find k.

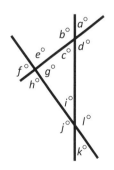

14.   If $g = 90$, what is $a + k$?

15.   If $f + k = 150$, find b.

1. **95:** We know that $x + y = 180$, since any acute angle formed by a transversal that cuts across two parallel lines is supplementary to any obtuse angle. Use the information given to set up a system of two equations with two variables:

$$\begin{aligned} x + y &= 180 \\ x - y &= 10 \\ \hline 2x &= 190 \\ x &= 95 \end{aligned}$$

2. **72:** Set up a ratio, using the unknown multiplier, a.

$$\frac{x}{y} = \frac{3a}{2a}$$

$180 = x + y = 3a + 2a = 5a$

$180 = 5a$

$a = 36$

$y = 2a = 2(36) = 72$

3. **140:** Use the fact that $x + y = 180$ to set up a system of two equations with two variables:

$$\begin{aligned} x + y = 180 \quad &\rightarrow \quad {-x - y} = -180 \\ & + \quad 2x + y = 320 \\ & \overline{ \quad x = 140} \end{aligned}$$

4. **120:** Use the fact that $x + y = 180$ to set up a system of two equations with two variables:

$$\begin{aligned} \frac{x}{x - y} = 2 \quad &\rightarrow \quad x - 2y = 0 \\ & - \quad x + y = 180 \\ & \overline{ -3y = -180} \\ & y = 60 \quad \rightarrow \quad \text{Therefore, } x = 120. \end{aligned}$$

5. **95:** Because a and d are vertical angles, they have the same measure: $a = d = 95°$. Likewise, since b and e are vertical angles, they have the same measure: $b = e$. Therefore, $b + d - e = d = 95°$.

6. **65:** Because c and f are vertical angles, they have the same measure: $c + f = 70$, so $c = f = 35$. Notice that b, c, and d form a straight line: $b + c + d = 180$. Substitute the known values of c and d into this equation:

$$\begin{aligned} b + 35 + 80 &= 180 \\ b + 115 &= 180 \\ b &= 65 \end{aligned}$$

7. ***b* and *d*, *a* and *e*, & *d* and *e*:** If a is complementary to b, then d (which is equal to a, since they are vertical angles), is also complementary to b. Likewise, if a is complementary to b, then a is also complementary to e (which is equal to b, since they are vertical angles). Finally, d and e must be complementary, since $d = a$ and $e = b$. You do not need to know the term "complementary," but you should be able to work with the concept (two angles adding up to 90°).

8. **315:** If $e = 45$, then the sum of all the other angles is $360 - 45 = 315°$.

9. **105:** We are told that $a + e = 150$. Since they are both acute angles formed by a transversal cutting across two parallel lines, they are also congruent. Therefore, $a = e = 75$. Any acute angle in this diagram is supplementary to any obtuse angle, so $75 + f = 180$, and $f = 105$.

10. **70:** We know that angles a and g are supplementary; their measures sum to 180. Therefore:

$$y + 3y + 20 = 180$$
$$4y = 160$$
$$y = 40$$

Angle f is congruent to angle g, so its measure is also $3y + 20$. The measure of angle $f = g = 3(40) + 20 = 140$. If $f = 2x$, then $140 = 2x \rightarrow x = 70$.

11. **70:** We are given the measure of one acute angle (a) and one obtuse angle (g). Since any acute angle in this diagram is supplementary to any obtuse angle, $11y + 4x - y = 180$, or $4x + 10y = 180$. Since angle d is congruent to angle a, we know that $5y + 2x - 20 = 4x - y$, or $2x - 6y = -20$. We can set up a system of two equations with two variables:

$$2x - 6y = -20 \ \rightarrow$$

$$\begin{aligned} -4x + 12y &= \ 40 \\ 4x + 10y &= 180 \\ \hline 22y &= 220 \\ y = 10; \ x &= 20 \end{aligned}$$

Since h is one of the acute angles, h has the same measure as a: $4x - y = 4(20) - 10 = 70$.

12. **68:** Because b and d are supplementary, $4x + 3y + 8 = 180$, or $4x + 3y = 172$. Since d and e are congruent, $3y + 8 = x + 2y$, or $x - y = 8$. We can set up a system of two equations with two variables:

$$x - y = 8 \qquad \rightarrow \qquad \begin{aligned} 4x + 3y &= 172 \\ 3x - 3y &= \ \ 24 \\ \hline 7x \quad\ \ &= 196 \\ x \quad\ \ &= 28; \ y = 20 \end{aligned}$$

Since h is congruent to d, $h = 3y + 8$, or $3(20) + 8 = 68$.

13. **40:** If $c + g = 140$, then $i = 40$, because there are $180°$ in a triangle. Since k is vertical to i, k is also = 40. Alternately, if $c + g = 140$, then $j = 140$, since j is an exterior angle of the triangle and is therefore equal to the sum of the two remote interior angles. Since k is supplementary to j, $k = 180 - 140 = 40$.

14. **90:** If $g = 90$, then the other two angles in the triangle, c and i, sum to 90. Since a and k are vertical angles to c and i, they sum to 90 as well.

15. **150:** Angles f and k are vertical to angles g and i. These two angles, then, must also sum to 150. Angle b, an exterior angle of the triangle, must be equal to the sum of the two remote interior angles g and i. Therefore, $b = 150$.

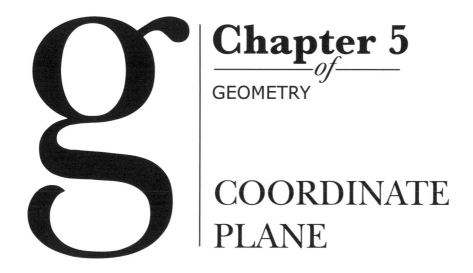

Chapter 5
of
GEOMETRY

COORDINATE
PLANE

In This Chapter . . .

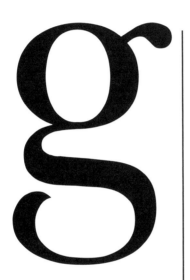

- The Slope of a Line
- The 4 Types of Slopes
- The Intercepts of a Line
- Slope-Intercept Equation: $y = mx + b$
- Horizontal and Vertical Lines
- Step by Step: From 2 Points to a Line
- The Distance Between 2 Points
- Positive and Negative Quadrants
- Perpendicular Bisectors
- The Intersection of Two Lines

THE COORDINATE PLANE

The coordinate plane is formed by a horizontal axis or reference line (the "**x-axis**") and a vertical axis (the "**y-axis**"), as shown here. These axes are each marked off like a number line, with both positive and negative numbers. The axes cross at right angles at the number zero on both axes.

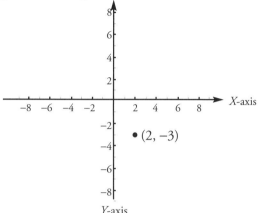

Points in the plane are identified by using an ordered pair of numbers, such as the one to the left: (2, −3). The first number in the ordered pair (2) is the **x-coordinate**, which corresponds to the point's horizontal location, as measured by the x-axis. The second number in the ordered pair (−3) is the **y-coordinate**, which corresponds to the point's vertical location, as indicated by the y-axis. The point (0, 0), where the axes cross, is called the **origin**.

A line in the plane is formed by the connection of two or more points. Notice that along the x-axis, the y-coordinate is zero. Likewise, along the y-axis, the x-coordinate is zero.

If the GMAT gives you coordinates with other variables, just match them to x and y. For instance, if you have point (a, b), a is the x-coordinate and b is the y-coordinate.

The Slope of a Line

The slope of a line is defined as "rise over run"—that is, how much the line <u>rises</u> vertically divided by how much the line <u>runs</u> horizontally.

The slope of a line can be determined by taking any two points on the line and (1) determining the "rise," or difference between their y-coordinates and (2) determining the "run," or difference between their x-coordinates.

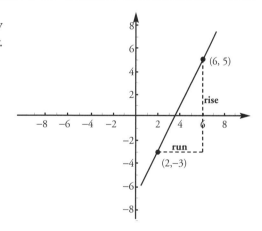

The slope is simply $\dfrac{\text{rise}}{\text{run}}$.

For example, in the diagram at the right, the line rises vertically from −3 to 5. This distance can be found by subtracting the y-coordinates: $5 - (-3) = 8$. Thus, the line rises 8 units. The line also runs horizontally from 2 to 6. This distance can be found by subtracting the x-coordinates: $6 - 2 = 4$. Thus, the line runs 4 units.

When we put together these results, we see that the slope of the line is: $\dfrac{\text{rise}}{\text{run}} = \dfrac{8}{4} = 2$.

Two other points on the line would typically have a different rise and run, but the slope would be the same. The "rise over run" would always be 2. A line has constant slope.

The slope of a line is equal to
$$\frac{\text{rise}}{\text{run}} = \frac{y_1 - y_2}{x_1 - x_2}$$

The 4 Types of Slopes

There are four types of slopes that a line can have:

Think of slope as walking from left to right. If you walked along a line with a positive slope, you would walk *up*.

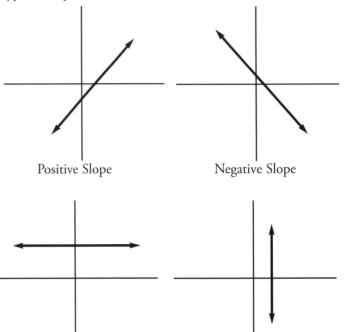

Positive Slope   Negative Slope

Zero Slope   Undefined Slope

A line with positive slope rises upward from left to right. A line with negative slope falls downward from left to right. A horizontal line has zero slope. A vertical line has undefined slope. Notice that the *x*-axis has zero slope, while the *y*-axis has undefined slope.

The Intercepts of a Line

A point where a line intersects a coordinate axis is called an **intercept**. There are two types of intercepts: the *x*-intercept, where the line intersects the *x*-axis, and the *y*-intercept, where the line intersects the *y*-axis.

The *x*-intercept is expressed using the ordered pair $(x, 0)$, where *x* is the point where the line intersects the *x*-axis. **The *x*-intercept is the point on the line at which $y = 0$.** In this diagram, the *x*-intercept is −4, as expressed by the ordered pair (−4, 0).

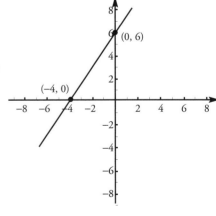

The *y*-intercept is expressed using the ordered pair $(0, y)$, where *y* is the point where the line intersects the *y*-axis. **The *y*-intercept is the point on the line at which $x = 0$.** In this diagram, the *y*-intercept is 6, as expressed by the ordered pair (0, 6).

To find *x*-intercepts, <u>plug in 0 for *y*</u>. To find *y*-intercepts, <u>plug in 0 for *x*</u>.

*Manhattan*GMAT*Prep
the new standard

Slope-Intercept Equation: y = mx + b

All lines can be written as equations in the form $y = mx + b$, where m represents the slope of the line and b represents the y-intercept of the line. This is a convenient form for graphing.

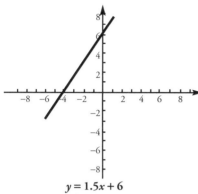

$y = 1.5x + 6$
The slope of the line is 1.5 (positive).
The y-intercept of the line is 6.

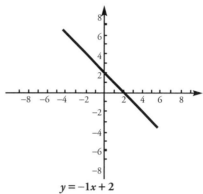

$y = -1x + 2$
The slope of the line is −1 (negative).
The y-intercept of the line is 2.

Linear equations represent lines in the coordinate plane. Linear equations often look like this: $Ax + By = C$, where A, B, and C are numbers. For instance, $6x + 3y = 18$ is a linear equation. Linear equations never involve terms such as x^2, $\sqrt{x}$, or xy. When you want to graph a linear equation, rewrite it in the slope-intercept form ($y = mx + b$). Then you can easily draw the line.

> What is the slope-intercept form for a line with the equation 6x + 3y = 18?

Rewrite the equation by solving for y as follows:

$$6x + 3y = 18$$
$$3y = 18 - 6x \qquad \text{Subtract } 6x \text{ from both sides}$$
$$y = 6 - 2x \qquad \text{Divide both sides by 3}$$
$$y = -2x + 6 \qquad \text{Thus, the } y\text{-intercept is } (0, 6), \text{ and the slope is } -2.$$

Horizontal and Vertical Lines

Horizontal and vertical lines are not expressed in the $y = mx + b$ form. Instead, they are expressed as simple, one-variable equations.

Horizontal lines are expressed in the form:
$y = $ *some number*, such as $y = 3$ or $y = 5$.
Vertical lines are expressed in the form:
$x = $ *some number*, such as $x = 4$ or $x = 7$.

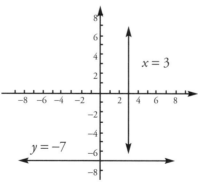

All the points on a vertical line have the same x- coordinate. This is why the equation of a vertical line is defined only by x. The y-axis itself corresponds to the equation $x = 0$. Likewise, all the points on a horizontal line have the same y-coordinate. This is why the equation of a horizontal line is defined only by y. The x-axis itself corresponds to the equation $y = 0$.

Vertical lines take the form $x = $ *some number*.
Horizontal lines take the form $y = $ *some number*.

Manhattan **GMAT** Prep
the new standard

Step by Step: From 2 Points to a Line

If you are given any two points on a line, you should be able to write an equation for that line in the form $y = mx + b$. Here is the step-by-step method:

Find the equation of the line containing the points $(5, -2)$ and $(3, 4)$.

FIRST: Find the slope of the line by calculating the rise over the run.

The rise is the difference between the y-coordinates, while the run is the difference between the x-coordinates. The sign of each difference is important, so subtract the x-coordinates and the y-coordinates in the same order.

> To find the equation of a line, you should start by finding its slope.

$$\frac{\text{rise}}{\text{run}} = \frac{y_1 - y_2}{x_1 - x_2} = \frac{-2 - 4}{5 - 3} = \frac{-6}{2} = -3 \qquad \text{The slope of the line is } -3.$$

SECOND: Plug the slope in for m in the slope-intercept equation.

$$y = -3x + b$$

THIRD: Solve for b, the y-intercept, by plugging the coordinates of one point into the equation. Either point's coordinates will work.

Plugging the point $(3, 4)$ into the equation (3 for x and 4 for y) yields the following:

$$4 = -3(3) + b$$
$$4 = -9 + b \qquad\qquad \text{The } y\text{-intercept of the line is 13.}$$
$$b = 13$$

FOURTH: Write the equation in the form $y = mx + b$.

$$y = -3x + 13 \qquad\qquad \text{This is the equation of the line.}$$

Note that sometimes the GMAT will only give you one point on the line, along with the y-intercept. This is the same thing as giving you two points on the line, because the y-intercept is a point! A y-intercept of 4 is the same as the ordered pair $(0, 4)$.

*Manhattan*GMAT*Prep
the new standard

The Distance Between 2 Points

The distance between any two points in the coordinate plane can be calculated by using the Pythagorean Theorem. For example:

What is the distance between the points (1, 3) and (7, −5)?

(1) Draw a right triangle connecting the points.

(2) Find the lengths of the two legs of the triangle by calculating the rise and the run.

The *y*-coordinate changes from 3 to −5, a difference of 8 (the vertical leg).

The *x*-coordinate changes from 1 to 7, a difference of 6 (the horizontal leg).

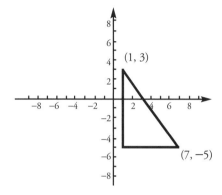

Draw a right triangle to find the distance between two points.

(3) Use the Pythagorean Theorem to calculate the length of the diagonal, which is the distance between the points.

$$6^2 + 8^2 = c^2$$
$$36 + 64 = c^2$$
$$100 = c^2$$
$$c = 10$$

The distance between the two points is 10 units.

Alternatively, to find the hypotenuse, we might have recognized this triangle as a variation of a 3−4−5 triangle (specifically, a 6−8−10 triangle).

Positive and Negative Quadrants

There are four quadrants in the coordinate plane, as shown in the diagram below.

Quadrant I contains only those points with a **positive** x-coordinate & a **positive** y-coordinate.

Quadrant II contains only those points with a **negative** x-coordinate & a **positive** y-coordinate.

Quadrant III contains only those points with a **negative** x-coordinate & a **negative** y-coordinate.

Quadrant IV contains only those points with a **positive** x-coordinate & a **negative** y-coordinate.

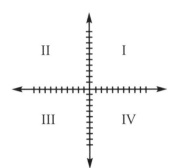

You do not need to memorize the numbers of the quadrants. The numbers will always be provided for you.

The GMAT sometimes asks you to determine which quadrants a given line passes through. For example:

Which quadrants does the line $2x + y = 5$ pass through?

(1) First, rewrite the line in the form $y = mx + b$.

$$2x + y = 5$$
$$y = 5 - 2x$$
$$y = -2x + 5$$

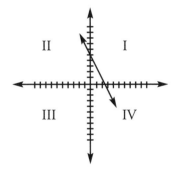

(2) Then sketch the line. Since $b = 5$, the y-intercept is the point (0, 5). The slope is −2, so the line slopes downward steeply to the right from the y-intercept. Although we do not know exactly where the line intersects the x-axis, we can now see that the line passes through quadrants I, II, and IV.

Alternatively, you can find two points on the line by setting x and y equal to zero in the original equation. In this way, you can find the x- and y- intercepts.

$$x = 0 \qquad\qquad y = 0$$
$$2x + y = 5 \qquad 2x + y = 5$$
$$2(0) + y = 5 \qquad 2x + (0) = 5$$
$$y = 5 \qquad\qquad x = 2.5$$

The points (0, 5) and (2.5, 0) are both on the line.

Now sketch the line, using the points you have identified. If you plot (0, 5) and (2.5, 0) on the coordinate plane, you can connect them to see the position of the line. Again, the line passes through quadrants I, II, and IV.

*Manhattan*GMAT*Prep

Perpendicular Bisectors

The perpendicular bisector of a line segment forms a 90° angle with the segment and divides the segment exactly in half. Questions about perpendicular bisectors are rare on the GMAT, but they do appear occasionally.

> If the coordinates of point *A* are (2, 2) and the coordinates of point *B* are (0, −2), what is the equation of the perpendicular bisector of line segment *AB*?

The key to solving perpendicular bisector problems is remembering this property: the perpendicular bisector has the **negative reciprocal slope** of the line segment it bisects. That is, the product of the two slopes is −1. (The only exception occurs when one line is horizontal and the other line is vertical, since vertical lines have undefined slopes).

<u>(1) Find the slope of segment *AB*.</u>

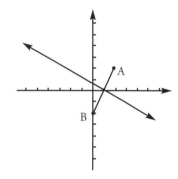

$$\text{slope} = \frac{\text{rise}}{\text{run}} = \frac{y_1 - y_2}{x_1 - x_2} = \frac{2 - (-2)}{2 - 0} = \frac{4}{2} = 2$$

The slope of *AB* is 2.

<u>(2) Find the slope of the perpendicular bisector of *AB*.</u>

Since perpendicular lines have negative reciprocal slopes, flip the fraction and change the sign to find the slope of the perpendicular bisector.

Again, the slope of *AB* is 2, or $\frac{2}{1}$.

Therefore, the slope of the perpendicular bisector of *AB* is $-\frac{1}{2}$.

Now we know that the equation of the perpendicular bisector has the following form:

$$y = -\frac{1}{2}x + b$$

However, we still need to find the value of *b* (the *y*-intercept). To do this, we will need to find one point on the perpendicular bisector. Then we will plug the coordinates of this point into the equation above.

Perpendicular lines have
negative reciprocal
slopes. That is, the
product of the two
slopes equals −1.

<u>(3) Find the midpoint of *AB*.</u>

The perpendicular bisector passes through the midpoint of *AB*. Thus, if we find the midpoint of *AB*, we will have found a point on the perpendicular bisector. Organize a chart such as the one shown below to find the coordinates of the midpoint. Simply write the *x*- and *y*-coordinates of *A* and *B*. The coordinates of the midpoint will be the numbers right in between each pair of *x*- and *y*-coordinates. In other words, the *x*-coordinate of the midpoint is the <u>average</u> of the *x*-coordinates of *A* and *B*. Likewise, the *y*-coordinate of the midpoint is the <u>average</u> of the *y*-coordinates of *A* and *B*. This process will yield the midpoint of any line segment.

	x	y
A	2	2
Midpoint	**1**	**0**
B	0	−2

<u>(4) Put the information together.</u>

To find the value of *b* (the *y*-intercept), substitute the coordinates of the midpoint for *x* and *y*.

$$0 = -\frac{1}{2}(1) + b$$

$$b = \frac{1}{2}$$

The perpendicular bisector of segment *AB* has the equation: $y = -\frac{1}{2}x + \frac{1}{2}$.

In summary, the following rules can be given:

- **<u>Parallel</u> lines have equal slopes.** $m_1 = m_2$.

- **<u>Perpendicular</u> lines have negative reciprocal slopes.** $\dfrac{-1}{m_1} = m_2$, or $m_1 \cdot m_2 = -1$.

- The midpoint between point A(x_1, y_1) and point B(x_2, y_2) is $\left(\dfrac{x_1 + x_2}{2}, \dfrac{y_1 + y_2}{2} \right)$.

> To find the midpoint of a line segment, find the midpoints of the *x*- and *y*- coordinates separately.

*Manhattan*GMAT*Prep
the new standard

The Intersection of Two Lines

Recall that a line in the coordinate plane is defined by a linear equation relating x and y. That is, if a point (x, y) lies on the line, then those values of x and y satisfy the equation. For instance, the point $(3, 2)$ lies on the line defined by the equation $y = 4x - 10$, since the equation is true when we plug in $x = 3$ and $y = 2$:

$$y = 4x - 10$$
$$2 = 4(3) - 10 = 12 - 10$$
$$2 = 2 \quad \text{TRUE}$$

On the other hand, the point $(7, 5)$ does not lie on that line, because the equation is false when we plug in $x = 7$ and $y = 5$:

$$y = 4x - 10$$
$$5 = 4(7) - 10 = 28 - 10 = 18? \quad \text{FALSE}$$

If two lines in a plane intersect in a single point, the coordinates of that point solve the equations of <u>both</u> lines.

So, what does it mean when two lines intersect in the coordinate plane? It means that at the point of intersection, BOTH equations representing the lines are true. That is, the pair of numbers (x, y) that represents the point of intersection solves BOTH equations. Finding this point of intersection is equivalent to solving a system of two linear equations. You can find the intersection by using algebra more easily than by graphing the two lines.

> At what point does the line represented by $y = 4x - 10$ intersect the line represented by $2x + 3y = 26$?

Since $y = 4x - 10$, replace y in the second equation with $4x - 10$ and solve for x:

$$2x + 3(4x - 10) = 26$$
$$2x + 12x - 30 = 26$$
$$14x = 56$$
$$x = 4$$

Now solve for y. You can use either equation, but the first one is more convenient:

$$y = 4x - 10$$
$$y = 4(4) - 10$$
$$y = 16 - 10 = 6$$

Thus, the point of intersection of the two lines is $(4, 6)$.

If two lines in a plane do not intersect, then the lines are parallel. If this is the case, there is NO pair of numbers (x, y) that satisfies both equations at the same time.

Two linear equations can represent two lines that intersect at a single point, or they can represent parallel lines that never intersect. There is one other possibility: the two equations might represent the same line. In this case, infinitely many points (x, y) along the line satisfy the two equations (which must actually be the same equation in two disguises).

*Manhattan*GMAT*Prep

Problem Set

1. A line has the equation $y = 3x + 7$. At which point will this line intersect the y-axis?

2. A line has the equation $x = \dfrac{y}{80} - 20$. At which point will this line intersect the x-axis?

3. A line has the equation $x = -2y + z$. If $(3, 2)$ is a point on the line, what is z?

4. What are the equations for the four lines that form the boundaries of the shaded area in the figure shown?

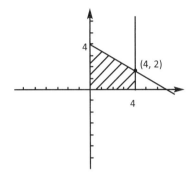

5. A line is represented by the equation $y = zx + 18$. If this line intersects the x-axis at $(-3, 0)$, what is z?

6. A line has a slope of 1/6 and intersects the x-axis at $(-24, 0)$. Where does this line intersect the y-axis?

7. A line has a slope of 3/4 and intersects the point $(-12, -39)$. At which point does this line intersect the x-axis?

8. The line represented by the equation $y = x$ is the perpendicular bisector of line segment AB. If A has the coordinates $(-3, 3)$, what are the coordinates of B?

9. What are the coordinates for the point on Line AB (see figure) that is three times as far from A as from B, and that is in between points A and B?

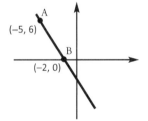

10. Which quadrants, if any, do not contain any points on the line represented by $x - y = 18$?

11. Which quadrants, if any, do not contain any points on the line represented by $x = 10y$?

12. Which quadrants, if any, contain points on the line $y = \dfrac{x}{1,000} + 1,000,000$?

13. Which quadrants, if any, contain points on the line represented by $x + 18 = 2y$?

14. What is the equation of the line shown to the right?

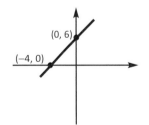

15. What is the intersection point of the lines defined by the equations $2x + y = 7$ and $3x - 2y = 21$?

1. **(0, 7):** A line intersects the y-axis at the y-intercept. Since this equation is written in slope-intercept form, the y-intercept is easy to identify: 7. Thus, the line intersects the y-axis at the point (0, 7).

2. **(−20, 0) :** A line intersects the x-axis at the x-intercept, or when the y-coordinate is equal to zero. Substitute zero for y and solve for x:
$$x = 0 - 20$$
$$x = -20$$

3. **7:** Substitute the coordinates (3, 2) for x and y and solve for z.
$$3 = -2(2) + z$$
$$3 = -4 + z$$
$$z = 7$$

4. $x = 0$, $x = 4$, $y = 0$, and $y = -\dfrac{1}{2}x + 4$:

The shaded area is bounded by 2 vertical lines: $x = 0$ AND $x = 4$. Notice that all the points on each line share the same x-coordinate. The shaded area is bounded by 1 horizontal line, the x-axis. The equation for the x-axis is $y = 0$. Finally, the shaded area is bounded by a slanted line. To find the equation of this line, first calculate the slope, using two points on the line: (0, 4) and (4, 2).

$$\text{slope} = \frac{\text{rise}}{\text{run}} = \frac{4 - 2}{0 - 4} = \frac{2}{-4} = -\frac{1}{2}$$

We can read the y-intercept from the graph; it is the point at which the line crosses the y-axis, or 4.

Therefore, the equation of this line is $y = -\dfrac{1}{2}x + 4$.

5. **6:** Substitute the coordinates (3, 2) for x and y and solve for z.
$$0 = z(-3) + 18$$
$$3z = 18$$
$$z = 6$$

6. **(0, 4):** Use the information given to find the equation of the line:

$$y = \frac{1}{6}x + b$$

$$0 = \frac{1}{6}(-24) + b$$

$$0 = -4 + b$$
$$b = 4$$

The variable b represents the y-intercept. Therefore, the line intersects the y-axis at (0, 4).

7. **(40, 0):** Use the information given to find the equation of the line:

$$y = \frac{3}{4}x + b$$

$$-39 = \frac{3}{4}(-12) + b$$
$$-39 = -9 + b$$
$$b = -30$$

The line intersects the x-axis when y = 0. Set y equal to zero and solve for x:

$$0 = \frac{3}{4}x - 30$$

$$\frac{3}{4}x = 30$$

$$x = 40$$

The line intersects the x-axis at (40, 0).

8. **(3, −3):** Perpendicular lines have negative inverse slopes. Therefore, if y = x is perpendicular to segment AB, we know that the slope of the perpendicular bisector is 1, and therefore the slope of segment AB is −1. The line containing segment AB takes the form of y = −x + b. To find the value of b, substitute the coordinates of A, (−3, 3), into the equation:

$$3 = -(-3) + b$$
$$b = 0$$

The line containing segment AB is y = −x.

Find the point at which the perpendicular bisector intersects AB by setting the two equations, y = x and y = −x, equal to each other:

$$x = -x$$
$$x = 0; y = 0$$

The two lines intersect at (0, 0), which is the midpoint of AB.

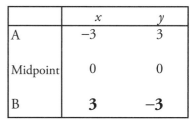

	x	y
A	−3	3
Midpoint	0	0
B	**3**	**−3**

Use a chart to find the coordinates of B.

9. **(−2.75, 1.5):** The point in question is 3 times farther from A than it is from B. We can represent this fact by labeling the point 3x units from A and x units from B, as shown, giving us a total distance of 4x between the two points. If we drop vertical lines from the point and from A to the x-axis, we get 2 similar triangles, the smaller of which is a quarter of the larger. (We can get this relationship from the fact that the larger triangle's hypotenuse is 4 times larger than the hypotenuse of the smaller triangle.)

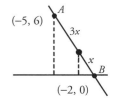

Manhattan **GMAT** Prep
the new standard

The horizontal distance between points A and B is 3 units (from -2 to -5). Therefore, $4x = 3$, and $x = 0.75$. The horizontal distance from B to the point is x, or 0.75 units. The x-coordinate of the point is 0.75 away from -2, or -2.75.

The vertical distance between points A and B is 6 units (from 0 to 6). Therefore, $4x = 6$, and $x = 1.5$. The vertical distance from B to the point is x, or 1.5 units. The y-coordinate of the point is 1.5 away from 0, or 1.5.

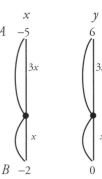

10. **II:** First, rewrite the line in slope-intercept form:
$$y = x - 18$$

Find the intercepts by setting x to zero and y to zero:
$$y = 0 - 18 \qquad\qquad 0 = x - 18$$
$$y = -18 \qquad\qquad x = 18$$

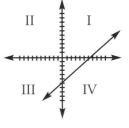

Plot the points: $(0, -18)$, and $(18, 0)$. From the sketch, we can see that the line does not pass through quadrant II.

11. **II and IV:** First, rewrite the line in slope-intercept form:

$$y = \frac{x}{10}$$

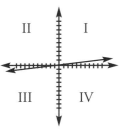

Notice from the equation that the y-intercept of the line is $(0,0)$. This means that the line crosses the y-intercept at the origin, so the x- and y-intercepts are the same. To find another point on the line, substitute any convenient number for x; in this case, 10 would be a convenient, or "smart," number.

$$y = \frac{10}{10} = 1 \qquad\qquad \text{The point } (10, 1) \text{ is on the line.}$$

Plot the points: $(0, 0)$ and $(10, 1)$. From the sketch, we can see that the line does not pass through quadrants II and IV.

12. **I, II, and III:** First, rewrite the line in slope-intercept form:
$$y = \frac{x}{1,000} + 1,000,000$$

Find the intercepts by setting x to zero and y to zero:

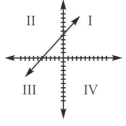

$$0 = \frac{x}{1,000} + 1,000,000 \qquad\qquad y = \frac{0}{1,000} + 1,000,000$$
$$x = -1,000,000,000 \qquad\qquad y = 1,000,000$$

Plot the points: $(-1,000,000,000, 0)$ and $(0, 1,000,000)$. From the sketch, we can see that the line passes through quadrants I, II, and III.

13. **I, II, and III:** First, rewrite the line in slope-intercept form:

$$y = \frac{x}{2} + 9$$

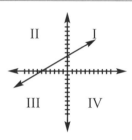

Find the intercepts by setting x to zero and y to zero:

$$0 = \frac{x}{2} + 9 \qquad\qquad y = \frac{0}{2} + 9$$

$$x = -18 \qquad\qquad\qquad y = 9$$

Plot the points: $(-18, 0)$ and $(0, 9)$. From the sketch, we can see that the line passes through quadrants I, II, and III.

14. $y = \frac{3}{2}x + 6$: First, calculate the slope of the line:

$$\text{slope} = \frac{\text{rise}}{\text{run}} = \frac{6 - 0}{0 - (-4)} = \frac{6}{4} = \frac{3}{2}$$

We can see from the graph that the line crosses the y-axis at $(0,6)$. The equation of the line is:

$$y = \frac{3}{2}x + 6$$

15. **(5, −3):** To find the coordinates of the point of intersection, solve the system of 2 linear equations. You could turn both equations into slope-intercept form and set them equal to each other, but it is easier is to multiply the first equation by 2 and then add the second equation:

$$2x + y = 7 \quad \text{(first equation)} \qquad\qquad 7x = 35 \quad \text{(sum of previous two equations)}$$
$$4x + 2y = 14 \quad \text{(multiply by 2)} \qquad\qquad\quad x = 5$$
$$3x - 2y = 21 \quad \text{(second equation)}$$

Now plug $x = 5$ into either equation:

$$2x + y = 7 \quad \text{(first equation)} \qquad\qquad 10 + y = 7$$
$$2(5) + y = 7 \qquad\qquad\qquad\qquad\qquad y = -3$$

Thus, the point $(5, -3)$ is the point of intersection. There is no need to graph the two lines and find the point of intersection manually.

*Manhattan*GMAT Prep
the new standard

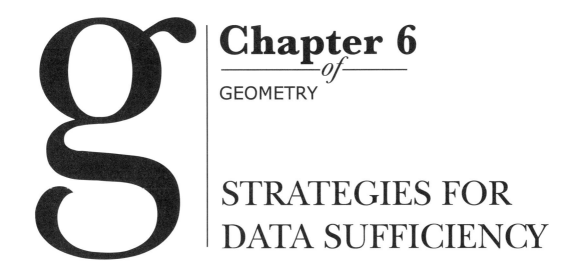

Chapter 6
of
GEOMETRY

STRATEGIES FOR
DATA SUFFICIENCY

In This Chapter . . .

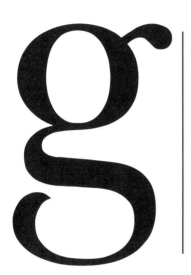

- Rephrasing: Access Useful Formulas and Rules
- Sample Rephrasings for Challenging Problems

Rephrasing: Access Useful Formulas and Rules

Geometry data sufficiency problems require you to identify the rules and formulas of geometry. For example, if you are given a problem about a circle, you should immediately access the rules and formulas you know that involve circles:

> Area of a circle $= \pi r^2$
> Circumference of a circle $= 2\pi r = \pi d$
> A central angle describes an arc that is proportional to a fractional part of 360°.
> An inscribed angle describes an arc that is proportional to a fractional part of 180°.

If *B* is the center of the circle to the right, what is the length of line segment *AC*?

(1) The area of sector *ABCD* is 4π
(2) The circumference of the circle is 8π

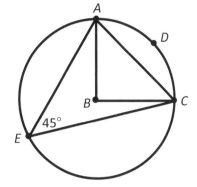

To solve Data Sufficiency problems in Geometry, apply the formulas and rules you have memorized.

(A)   Statement (1) ALONE is sufficient, but statement (2) alone is not sufficient.
(B)   Statement (2) ALONE is sufficient, but statement (1) alone is not sufficient.
(C)   BOTH statements TOGETHER are sufficient, but NEITHER statement ALONE is sufficient.
(D)   EACH statement ALONE is sufficient.
(E)   Statements (1) and (2) together are NOT sufficient.

Always start by focusing on the question itself. Do not jump to the statements before first attempting to rephrase the question into something easier. You need to process the information that you ALREADY KNOW (from the question and diagram) before diving into NEW information (from the statements).

The diagram shows that $\angle AEC$ (an inscribed angle that intercepts arc *ADC*) is 45°.

Therefore, using the relationship between an inscribed angle and a central angle, we know that $\angle ABC$ (a central angle that also intercepts arc *ADC*) must be 90°.

Thus, triangle *ABC* is a right triangle.

The question asks us to find the length of line segment *AC*, which is the hypotenuse of the right triangle. In order to find the length of hypotenuse *AC*, we must determine the length of the legs of the triangle. Notice that each leg of the triangle (*BA* and *BC*) is a radius of the circle.

Thus, this question can be rephrased: **What is the radius of the circle?**

You should know two circle formulas that include the radius: the formula for area and the formula for circumference.

Statement (1) tells us the area of a sector of the circle. Since the sector described is one quarter of the circle, we will be able to determine the area of the entire circle using a proportion. Given the area of the circle, we can find the radius.

Thus, statement (1) alone is sufficient to answer our rephrased question.

Statement (2) tells us the circumference of the circle. Using the formula for circumference, we can determine the radius of the circle.

Thus, statement (2) alone is sufficient to answer our rephrased question.

The answer to this data sufficiency problem is (D): EACH statement ALONE is sufficient.

Try to determine whether each statement provides enough information to answer your *rephrased* question.

Rephrasing: Challenge Short Set

In Chapters 7 and 9, you will find lists of Geometry problems that have appeared on past official GMAT exams. These lists refer to problems from three books published by the Graduate Management Admission Council® (the organization that develops the official GMAT exam):

The Official Guide for GMAT Review, 12th Edition
The Official Guide for GMAT Quantitative Review
The Official Guide for GMAT Quantitative Review, 2nd Edition

<u>Note</u>: The two editions of the Quant Review book largely overlap. Use one OR the other. The questions contained in these three books are the property of The Graduate Management Admission Council, which is not affiliated in any way with Manhattan GMAT.

As you work through the Data Sufficiency problems listed at the end of Part I and Part II, be sure to focus on *rephrasing*. If possible, try to *rephrase* each question into its simplest form *before* looking at the two statements. In order to rephrase, focus on figuring out the specific information that is absolutely necessary to answer the question. After rephrasing the question, you should also try to *rephrase* each of the two statements, if possible. Rephrase each statement by simplifying the given information into its most basic form.

In order to help you practice rephrasing, we have taken a set of generally difficult Data Sufficiency problems on *The Official Guide* problem list (these are the problem numbers listed in the "Challenge Short Set" on page 113) and have provided you with our own sample rephrasings for each question and statement. In order to evaluate how effectively you are using the rephrasing strategy, you can compare your rephrased questions and statements to our own rephrasings that appear below. Questions and statements that are significantly rephrased appear in **bold**.

Rephrasings from *The Official Guide For GMAT Review, 12th Edition*

The questions and statements that appear below are only our *rephrasings*. The original questions and statements can be found by referencing the problem numbers below in the Data Sufficiency section of *The Official Guide for GMAT Review, 12th Edition* (pages 272–288).

<u>Note</u>: Problem numbers preceded by "D" refer to questions in the Diagnostic Test chapter of *The Official Guide for GMAT Review, 12th Edition* (pages 24–26).

34.   **What is the diameter of each can?**

    (1) $r = 4$
        $d = 8$

    (2) $6d = 48$
        $d = 8$

56.   There are $180°$ in a triangle: $x + y + z = 180$
                                          $z = 180 - (x + y)$

    What is the value of $x + y$?

    (1) $x + y = 139$

    (2) $y + z = 108$

94.   **What is the value of m?**

    (1) $m = 1 - m$
        $m = 1/2$

    (2) $7 = 2m + b$

117.   Area of large circle − Area of small circle = ?

    $\pi r_{large}^{2} - \pi r_{small}^{2} = ?$

    $\pi(r_{large}^{2} - r_{small}^{2}) = ?$

    Rephrasing most likely to be useful at this point:

    What are the values of r_{large} and r_{small}?

    (1) $r_{small} = 3$ and $r_{large} = 3 + 2$

    (2) $r_{large} = 1 + 4 = 5$

        $2r_{large} = 10$ $DE = 4$ so $AD = 6$
                                        $= 2r_{small}$
                                $r_{small} = 3$

121. $3y \le -2x + 6$

   $y \le \dfrac{-2}{3}x + 2$

   Is $s \le \dfrac{-2}{3}r + 2$?

   Is (r, s) in the shaded region?

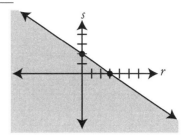

   (1) $2s = -3r + 6$

   $s = \dfrac{-3}{2}r + 3$

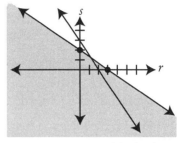

Possible (r, s) points
are on this line.

   (2)

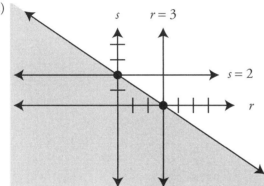

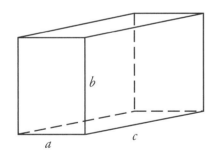

Possible (r, s) points
are below this line.

Possible (r, s) points
are to the left of this
line.

122.

What is the value of abc?

   (1) $ab = 15$ and $bc = 24$

   (2) $ac = 40$

132. $(180 - x) + (180 - y) + (180 - z) + (180 - w) = 360$

   $720 - (x + y + z + w) = 360$

   $360 = x + y + z + w$

   $360 - (z + w) = x + y$

   (1) $w = 95$

   (2) $z = 125$

144.   **What is the length of one side of triangle _D_?**

      (1) **The length of the height of triangle _D_ is 3.**

      (2) **The length of the base of triangle _D_ is $\dfrac{8}{3}$.**

148. $x + x + 3x + (x + 60) = ?$ $x > 0$, since it represents a length

      $6x + 60 = ?$

      What is the value of _x_?

      (1) $x = 120$ or $x + 60 = 120$ or $3x = 120$
                            $x = 60$ $x = 40$

      (2) $3x > x$ x is the measure of the 2 shortest sides.
          $x + 60 > x$ The $3x$ side cannot be twice as long as an x side (it's three times as long).
                              So, $x + 60 = 2x$
                                  $60 = x$

157.

                $x^2 + y^2 = 100$

                $x + y + 10 = ?$
                $x + y = ?$

      (1) $\dfrac{xy}{2} = 25$ This can also be achieved by substitution:

          $xy = 50$

          $2xy = 100$ $y = \dfrac{50}{x}$

         $x^2 + y^2 + 2xy = 100 + 100 = 200$ $x^2 + \left(\dfrac{50}{x}\right)^2 = 100$

         $(x + y)^2 = 200$ $x^2 + \dfrac{2500}{x^2} = 100$

         $x + y = \sqrt{200}$ $x^4 - 100x^2 + 2500 = 0$

                                    $(x^2 - 50)(x^2 - 50) = 0$

      (2) $x = y$ $x^2 = 50$

         $2x^2 = 100$ $x = \sqrt{50}$

          $x^2 = 50$ $y = \dfrac{50}{\sqrt{50}} = \sqrt{50}$

          $x = \sqrt{50} = y$ $x + y = 2\sqrt{50}$ $(= \sqrt{200})$

         $x + y = 2\sqrt{50}$

160. $C = 2\pi r$
        What is the radius?   OR
        Arc lengths are determined by central angles.

Thus, the length of arc $XYZ = \dfrac{90}{360} = \dfrac{1}{4}$ of the circumference.

What is the length of arc *XYZ*?

(1) Triangle *OXZ* is a 45–45–90 triangle with sides in the ratio of $1 : 1 : \sqrt{2}$, and each of the shorter legs is a radius of the circle. Thus, the perimeter is $r + r + \sqrt{2}r$. Using the value for the perimeter given in statement (1), solve for the radius:

$r = 10$

(2) arc $XYZ = 5\pi$

164.   The distance of a point to the origin can be determined with the Pythagorean Theorem.

Does $r^2 + s^2 = u^2 + v^2$?

(1) $s = -r + 1$

(2) $v = 1 - s$ AND $u = 1 - r$

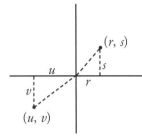

(COMBINED)
$v = 1 - (-r + 1)$ AND $u = 1 - r$
$v = r + 2$

Using substitution, we can answer the rephrased question.

173.   The large triangle (*PQR*) is inscribed in a semi-circle, and its hypotenuse (*PR*) is the diameter of the semi-circle. Therefore, triangle *PQR* is a right triangle; its right angle is at point *Q*.

Now we have one large right triangle (*PQR*) and two small right triangles (*PSQ* and *RSQ*). Notice that triangle *PQR* and triangle *PSQ* share two angles in common (angle *w* and a right angle). Since the sum of the angles in any triangle is 180 degrees, the third angle in each of these triangles must also be congruent. Therefore, these triangles are similar.

The same logic applies for triangle *PQR* and triangle *RSQ*. These two triangles are similar as well.

Since the large triangle *PQR* is similar to both of the smaller triangles, *PSQ* and *RSQ*, then these two smaller triangles must also be similar to each other. Therefore, knowing any pair of corresponding sides will give us the proportions of the other pairs of corresponding sides.

What is *a*?   OR   What is *b*?

(1) $a = 4$

(2) $b = 1$

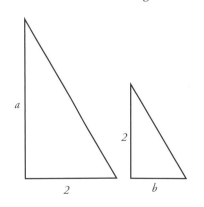

D39. *x*-intercept is the point on line where $y = 0$.

At point (x, 0) on line k, is x positive?

(1) Slope = distance between any 2 points on line: $-5 = \dfrac{rise}{run} = \dfrac{y_2 - y_1}{x_2 - x_1}$

Plug in two points on line k: (x, 0) and (-5, r)

$$-5 = \frac{r - 0}{-5 - x} = \frac{r}{-5 - x}$$

$$25 + 5x = r$$

$$x = \frac{r - 25}{5}$$

x is positive if r is greater than 25

(2) $r > 0$

D48.

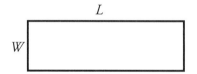

What is $2L + 2W$?   OR   **What is $L + W$?**

(1)

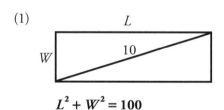

$L^2 + W^2 = 100$

(2) $LW = 48$

Rephrasings from *The Official Guide for GMAT Quantitative Review, 2nd Edition*

The questions and statements that appear below are only our *rephrasings*. The original questions and statements can be found by referencing the problem numbers below in the Data Sufficiency section of *The Official Guide for GMAT Quantitative Review, 2nd Edition* (pages 152–163). First Edition numbers are included in parentheses. Problems unique to one edition are so indicated.

59.
(58.)
Circumference of a circle $= 2\pi r$

Number of rotations $= \dfrac{100}{2\pi r}$

What is the value of *r*?

(1) diameter = 0.5 meter

(2) speed = 20 rotations per minute

72.
(70.)
What is the measure of angle *ABC*? OR

What are the measures of *ABX*, *XBY*, and *YBC*?

(1) *ABX* = *XBY* **AND** *XBY* = *YBC*
    ABX* = *XBY* = *YBC

(2) *ABX* = 40°

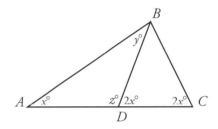

91.
(87.)
TUV is a 45–45–90 right triangle.   *RUV* is a 30–60–90 right triangle.
TU = *RS*

What is the length of the base of each of these triangles?   OR
What is the length of the hypotenuse these triangles share?   OR
(BEST): What is the length of any side in either triangle?
**Note that knowing 1 side allows us to solve for all other sides.

(1) *TU* = 10 m

(2) *RV* = 5 m

95.
(91.)
Let *r* = the radius of the smaller region.
Let *R* = the radius of the larger region.
What is *R*?

(1) $\pi r^2 + \pi R^2 = 90\pi$
    $r^2 + R^2 = 90$

(2) *R* = 3*r*

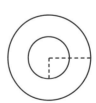

114.   **What is lw?**
(109.)

     (1) $l + w = 6$
         $(l + w)^2 = 36$
         $l^2 + 2lw + w^2 = 36$

     (2) $l^2 + w^2 = 20$

     (COMBINED)

$$\begin{aligned} l^2 + 2lw + w^2 &= 36 \\ -\quad l^2 \qquad\;\; + w^2 &= 20 \\ \hline 2lw \qquad\quad &= 16 \\ lw &= 8 \end{aligned}$$

123.   Name angles y and z as shown in the figure.
(117.)

     $2x + z = 180$ OR $z = 180 - 2x$
     $x + y + z = 180$ OR $z = 180 - (x + y)$
     Therefore, $2x = x + y$ OR $x = y$. Thus, $AD = BD$.

     We also know that $BD = BC$.
     Therefore, $AD = BD = BC$.

     What is the length of BC, BD, or AD?

     (1) $AD = 6$

     (2) $x = 36$

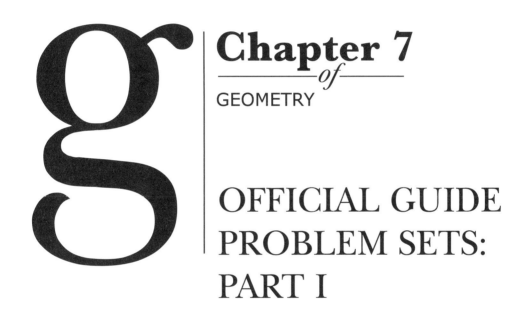

Chapter 7
of
GEOMETRY

OFFICIAL GUIDE
PROBLEM SETS:
PART I

In This Chapter . . .

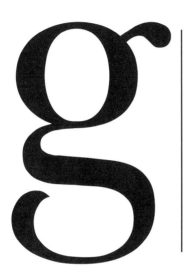

- Geometry Problem Solving List from *The Official Guides:* PART I
- Geometry Data Sufficiency List from *The Official Guides:* PART I

Practicing with REAL GMAT Problems

Now that you have completed Part I of GEOMETRY, it is time to test your skills on problems that have actually appeared on real GMAT exams over the past several years.

The problem sets that follow are composed of questions from three books published by the Graduate Management Admission Council® (the organization that develops the official GMAT exam):

The Official Guide for GMAT Review, 12th Edition
The Official Guide for GMAT Quantitative Review
The Official Guide for GMAT Quantitative Review, 2nd Edition
Note: The two editions of the Quant Review book largely overlap. Use one OR the other.

These books contain quantitative questions that have appeared on past official GMAT exams. (The questions contained therein are the property of The Graduate Management Admission Council, which is not affiliated in any way with Manhattan GMAT.)

Although the questions in the Official Guides have been "retired" (they will not appear on future official GMAT exams), they are great practice questions.

In order to help you practice effectively, we have categorized every problem in The Official Guides by topic and subtopic. On the following pages, you will find two categorized lists:

(1) **Problem Solving:** Lists EASIER Problem Solving Geometry questions contained in *The Official Guides* and categorizes them by subtopic.

(2) **Data Sufficiency:** Lists EASIER Data Sufficiency Geometry questions contained in *The Official Guides* and categorizes them by subtopic.

The remaining *Official Guide* problems are listed at the end of Part II of this book. **Do not forget about the Part II list!**

Each book in Manhattan GMAT's 8-book strategy series contains its own *Official Guide* lists that pertain to the specific topics taught in that particular book. If you complete all the practice problems contained in the *Official Guide* lists in each of the 8 Manhattan GMAT strategy books, you will have completed every single question published in *The Official Guides*.

Problem Solving: Part I

from *The Official Guide for GMAT Review, 12th Edition* (pages 20–23 & 152–185), *The Official Guide for GMAT Quantitative Review* (pages 62–85), and *The Official Guide for GMAT Quantitative Review, 2nd Edition* (pages 62–86). <u>Note</u>: The two editions of the Quant Review book largely overlap. Use one OR the other.

Solve each of the following problems in a notebook, making sure to demonstrate how you arrived at each answer by showing all of your work and computations. If you get stuck on a problem, look back at the GEOMETRY strategies and content contained in this guide to assist you.

<u>Note</u>: Problem numbers preceded by "D" refer to questions in the Diagnostic Test chapter of *The Official Guide for GMAT Review, 12th Edition* (pages 20–23).

GENERAL SET – GEOMETRY
Polygons
> *12th Edition*: 4, 16, 18, 102, 113
> *Quantitative Review*: 12, 22, 139 OR *2nd Edition*: 15, 24, 139

Triangles and Diagonals
> *12th Edition*: 48, 145, 147, 152
> *Quantitative Review*: 77 OR *2nd Edition*: 71, 76

Circles and Cylinders
> *12th Edition*: 33, 160, D5, D20
> *Quantitative Review*: 31 OR *2nd Edition*: 33

Lines and Angles
> *12th Edition*: 53, 62, D10
> *Quantitative Review*: 28 OR *2nd Edition*: 7, 30

Coordinate Plane
> *12th Edition*: 9, 25, 39, 88
> *Quantitative Review*: 19, 123 OR *2nd Edition*: 21, 83, 102, 123

Remember, there are more Official Guide problems listed at the end of Part II.

Data Sufficiency: Part I

from *The Official Guide for GMAT Review, 12th Edition* (pages 24–26 & 272–288), *The Official Guide for GMAT Quantitative Review* (pages 149–157), and *The Official Guide for GMAT Quantitative Review, 2nd Edition* (pages 152–163).

Note: The two editions of the Quant Review book largely overlap. Use one OR the other.

Solve each of the following problems in a notebook, making sure to demonstrate how you arrived at each answer by showing all of your work and computations. If you get stuck on a problem, look back at the GEOMETRY strategies and content contained in this guide to assist you.

Practice REPHRASING both the questions and the statements by using variables and constructing equations. The majority of data sufficiency problems can be rephrased; however, if you have difficulty rephrasing a problem, try testing numbers to solve it. It is especially important that you familiarize yourself with the directions for data sufficiency problems, and that you memorize the 5 fixed answer choices that accompany all data sufficiency problems.

Note: Problem numbers preceded by "D" refer to questions in the Diagnostic Test chapter of *The Official Guide for GMAT Review, 12th edition* (pages 24–26).

GENERAL SET – GEOMETRY
Polygons
> *12th Edition*: 18, 47, 122
> *Quantitative Review*: 4, 59, 84 OR *2nd Edition*: 4, 60, 88

Triangles and Diagonals
> *12th Edition*: 20, 56, 74, D28
> *Quantitative Review*: 19, 64, 87, 109 OR *2nd Edition*: 19, 43, 65, 91, 114, 123

Circles and Cylinders
> *12th Edition*: 29, 34, 42, 96, 114
> *Quantitative Review*: 57, 58, 91, 95 OR *2nd Edition*: 58, 59, 95, 99

Lines and Angles
> *12th Edition*: 91
> *Quantitative Review*: 70 OR *2nd Edition*: 72

Coordinate Plane
> *12th Edition*: 75, 94
> *Quantitative Review*: 14 OR *2nd Edition*: 22

Remember, there are more Official Guide problems listed at the end of Part II.

PART II: ADVANCED

This part of the book covers various advanced topics within *Geometry*. This advanced material may not be necessary for all students. Attempt Part II only after you have completed Part I and are comfortable with its content.

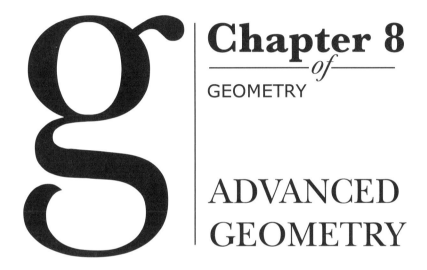

Chapter 8
of
GEOMETRY

ADVANCED GEOMETRY

In This Chapter . . .

ADVANCED GEOMETRY

Typically, difficult geometry problems draw on the <u>same</u> geometric principles as easier problems. The GMAT usually makes problems more difficult by adding steps. For instance, to solve Problem Solving #145 in *The Official Guide for GMAT Quantitative Review, 2nd Edition*, you have to complete several steps, using both Triangle concepts and Circle concepts. However, once you have labeled the diagram appropriately, each step is itself straightforward. Likewise, Problem Solving #229 in *The Official Guide for GMAT Review, 12th Edition* does not contain fundamentally difficult coordinate-plane geometry. What makes #229 hard is its hybrid nature: it is a Combinatorics problem in a Coordinate-Plane disguise.

All that said, a few miscellaneous topics in geometry may be called advanced. These topics rarely appear on easier problems.

Maximum Area of Polygons

In some problems, the GMAT may require you to determine the maximum or minimum area of a given figure. This condition could be stated *explicitly*, as in Problem Solving questions ("What is the maximum area of…?"), or *implicitly*, as in Data Sufficiency questions ("Is the area of rectangle ABCD less than 30?"). Following are two shortcuts that can help you optimize certain problems quickly.

Maximum Area of a Quadrilateral

Perhaps the best-known maximum area problem is to maximize the area of a *quadrilateral* (usually a rectangle) with a *fixed perimeter*. If a quadrilateral has a fixed perimeter, say, 36 inches, it can take a variety of shapes:

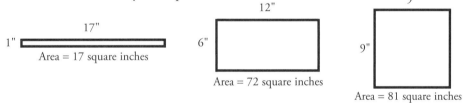

| 17" | 12" | 9" |
| Area = 17 square inches | Area = 72 square inches | Area = 81 square inches |

Of these figures, the one with the largest area is the square. This is a general rule: **Of all quadrilaterals with a given perimeter, the SQUARE has the largest area.** This is true even in cases involving non-integer lengths. For instance, of all quadrilaterals with a perimeter of 25 feet, the one with the largest area is a square with 25/4 = 6.25 feet per side.

This principle can also be turned around to yield the following corollary: **Of all quadrilaterals with a given area, the SQUARE has the minimum perimeter.**

Both of these principles can be generalized for *n* sides: a regular polygon with all sides equal (and pushed outward if necessary) will maximize area for a given perimeter and minimize perimeter for a given area.

Maximum Area of a Parallelogram or Triangle

Another common optimization problem involves maximizing the area of a *triangle or parallelogram with given side lengths.*

For instance, there are many triangles with two sides 3 and 4 units long. Imagine that the two sides of length 3 and 4 are on a hinge. The third side can have various lengths:

If you have a given amount of fence (perimeter) and want to build the biggest possible rectangular enclosure, make a square.

*Manhattan*GMAT*Prep
the new standard

There are many corresponding parallelograms with two sides 3 and 4 units long:

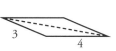   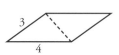

If you are given two sides of a triangle or parallelogram and you want to maximize the area, establish those sides as the base and height, and make the angle between them 90°.

The area of a triangle is given by $A = \dfrac{1}{2}bh$, and the area of a parallelogram is given by $A = bh$. Because both of these formulas involve the perpendicular height h, the maximum area of each figure is achieved when the 3-unit side is perpendicular to the 4-unit side, so that the height is 3 units. All the other figures have lesser heights. (Note that in this case, the triangle of maximum area is the famous 3–4–5 right triangle.) If the sides are not perpendicular, then the figure is squished, so to speak.

The general rule is this: **if you are given two sides of a triangle or parallelogram, you can maximize the area by placing those two sides PERPENDICULAR to each other.**

Since the rhombus is simply a special case of a parallelogram, this rule holds for rhombuses as well. All sides of a rhombus are equal. Thus, you can maximize the area of a rhombus with a given side length by making the rhombus into a square.

Function Graphs and Quadratics

We can think of the slope-intercept form of a linear equation as a function:
$y = f(x) = mx + b$. That is, we input the x-coordinate into the function $f(x) = mx + b$, and the output is the y-coordinate of the point that we plot on the line.

We can apply this process more generally. For instance, imagine that $y = f(x) = x^2$. Then we can generate the graph for $f(x)$ by plugging in a variety of values for x and getting values for y. The points (x, y) that we find lie on the graph of $y = f(x) = x^2$.

x	$f(x) = y$	Point
-3	$(-3)^2 = 9$	$(-3, 9)$
-2	$(-2)^2 = 4$	$(-2, 4)$
-1	$(-1)^2 = 1$	$(-1, 1)$
0	$0^2 = 0$	$(0, 0)$
1	$1^2 = 1$	$(1, 1)$
2	$2^2 = 2$	$(2, 4)$
3	$3^2 = 9$	$(3, 9)$

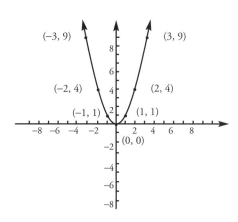

This curved graph is called a **parabola**. Any function of the form $f(x) = ax^2 + bx + c$, where a, b, and c are constants, is called a **quadratic function** and can be plotted as a parabola in the coordinate plane. Depending on the value of a, the curve will have different shapes:

Positive value for a Curve opens upward
Negative value for a Curve opens downward

Large $|a|$ (absolute value)   Narrow curve
Small $|a|$ Wide curve

The parabola will always open upward or downward.

The most important questions you will be asked about the parabola are these:

(1) How many times does the parabola touch the x-axis?
(2) If the parabola does touch the x-axis, where does it touch?

In other words, how many x-intercepts are there, and what are they?

The reason these questions are important is that the x-axis is the line representing $y = 0$. In other words, the parabola touches the x-axis at those values of x that make $f(x) = 0$.

Therefore, these values solve the quadratic equation given by $f(x) = ax^2 + bx + c = 0$.

You can solve for zero by factoring and solving the equation directly. Alternatively, you might plug in points and draw the parabola. Finally, for some very difficult problems, you can use the quadratic formula:

$$x = \frac{-b \pm \sqrt{b^2 - 4ac}}{2a}$$ One solution is $\dfrac{-b + \sqrt{b^2 - 4ac}}{2a}$, and the other is $\dfrac{-b - \sqrt{b^2 - 4ac}}{2a}$.

The vast majority of GMAT quadratic problems can be solved <u>without</u> using the quadratic formula. If you do apply this formula, the advantage is that you can quickly tell how many solutions the equation has by looking at just one part: the expression under the radical sign, $b^2 - 4ac$. This expression is known as the **discriminant**, because it discriminates or distinguishes three cases for the number of solutions to the equation, as follows:

(1) If $b^2 - 4ac > 0$, then the square root operation yields a positive number. The quadratic formula produces <u>two roots</u> of the quadratic equation. This means that the parabola crosses the x-axis twice and has two x-intercepts.

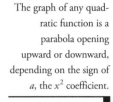

The graph of any quadratic function is a parabola opening upward or downward, depending on the sign of a, the x^2 coefficient.

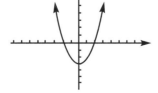

(2) If $b^2 - 4ac = 0$, then the square root operation yields zero. The quadratic formula only produces <u>one root</u> of the quadratic equation. This means that the parabola just touches the x-axis once and has just one x-intercept.

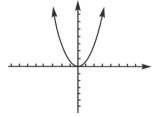

(3) If $b^2 - 4ac < 0$, then the square root operation cannot be performed. This means that the quadratic formula produces <u>no roots</u> of the quadratic equation, and the parabola never touches the x-axis (it has no x-intercepts).

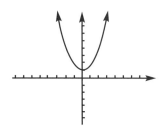

The number of x-intercepts of a parabola is determined by the sign of the **discriminant**.

It is possible for the GMAT to ask you to graph other non-linear functions of x. The following points lie at the heart of all problems involving graphs of other non-linear functions, as well as lines and parabolas.

(1) If a point lies on the graph, then you can plug its coordinates into the equation $y = f(x)$. Conversely, if a value of x and a value of y satisfy the equation $y = f(x)$, then the point (x, y) lies on the graph of $f(x)$.

(2) To find x-intercepts, find the values of x for which $y = f(x) = 0$.

(3) To find y-intercepts, set $x = 0$ and find $y = f(0)$.

Problem Set (Advanced)

1. What is the maximum possible area of a quadrilateral with a perimeter of 80 centimeters?

2. What is the minimum possible perimeter of a quadrilateral with an area of 1,600 square feet?

3. What is the maximum possible area of a parallelogram with one side of length 2 meters and a perimeter of 24 meters?

4. What is the maximum possible area of a triangle with a side of length 7 units and another side of length 8 units?

5. The lengths of the two shorter legs of a right triangle add up to 40 units. What is the maximum possible area of the triangle?

6. What is x in the diagram below?

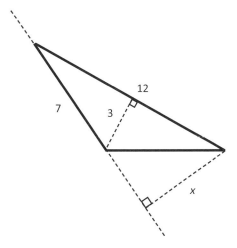

7. The line represented by the equation $y = -2x + 6$ is the perpendicular bisector of the line segment AB. If A has the coordinates (7, 2), what are the coordinates for B?

8. How many x-intercepts does $f(x) = x^2 + 3x + 3$ have?

1. **400 cm²:** The quadrilateral with maximum area for a given perimeter is a square, which has four equal sides. Therefore, the square that has a perimeter of 80 centimeters has sides of length 20 centimeters each. Since the area of a square is the side length squared, the area = (20 cm)(20 cm) = 400 cm².

2. **160 ft:** The quadrilateral with minimum perimeter for a given area is a square. Since the area of a square is the side length squared, we can solve the equation $x^2 = 1,600$ ft² for the side length x, yielding $x = 40$ ft. The perimeter, which is four times the side length, is (4)(40 ft) = 160 ft.

3. **20 m²:** If one side of the parallelogram is 2 meters long, then the opposite side must also be 2 meters long. We can solve for the unknown sides, which are equal in length, by writing an equation for the perimeter: $24 = 2(2) + 2x$, with x as the unknown side. Solving, we get $x = 10$ meters. The parallelogram with these dimensions and maximum area is a <u>rectangle</u> with 2-meter and 10-meter sides. Thus the maximum possible area of the figure is (2 m)(10 m) = 20 m².

4. **28 square units:** A triangle with two given sides has maximum area if these two sides are placed at right angles to each other. For this triangle, one of the given sides can be considered the base, and the other side can be considered the height (because they meet at a right angle). Thus we plug these sides into the formula

$$A = \frac{1}{2}bh: \quad A = \frac{1}{2}(7)(8) = 28.$$

5. **200 square units:** You can think of a right triangle as half of a rectangle. Constructing this right triangle with legs adding to 40 is equivalent to constructing the rectangle with a perimeter of 80. Since the area of the triangle is half that of the rectangle, you can use the previously mentioned technique for maximizing the area of a rectangle: of all rectangles with a given perimeter, the *square* has the greatest area. The desired rectangle is thus a 20 by 20 square, and the right triangle has area (½)(20)(20) = 200 units.

6. **36/7:** We can calculate the area of the triangle, using the side of length 12 as the base:

    (1/2)(12)(3) = 18

Next, we use the side of length 7 as the base and write the equation for the area:

    (1/2)(7)(x) = 18

Now solve for x, the unknown height.
    $7x = 36$
    $x = 36/7$

You could also solve this problem using the Pythagorean Theorem, but the process is *much* harder.

7. **(−1, −2):** If $y = -2x + 6$ is the perpendicular bisector of segment AB, then the line containing segment AB must have a slope of 0.5 (the negative inverse of −2). We can represent this line with the equation $y = 0.5x + b$. Substitute the coordinates (7, 2) into the equation to find the value of b.
    $2 = 0.5(7) + b.$
    $b = -1.5$

	x	y
A	7	2
Midpoint	3	0
B	−1	−2

The line containing AB is $y = 0.5x - 1.5$.

Find the point at which the perpendicular bisector intersects AB by setting the two equations, $y = -2x + 6$ and $y = 0.5x - 1.5$, equal to each other.

$$-2x + 6 = 0.5x - 1.5$$
$$2.5x = 7.5$$
$$x = 3; y = 0$$

The two lines intersect at (3, 0), which is the midpoint of AB.

Use a chart to find the coordinates of B.

8. **None:** There are three ways to solve this equation. The first is to attempt to factor the quadratic equation to find solutions. Since no two integers multiply to 3 and add to 3, this strategy fails.

<table>
<tr><td rowspan="6">The second approach is to pick numbers for x, solve for $f(x)$ (plotted as y in the coordinate plane), and plot these (x, y) pairs to determine the shape of the parabola. An example of this technique is displayed to the right.</td></tr>
</table>

x	$x^2 + 3x + 3 = y$	Point
-3	$9 - 9 + 3 = 3$	$(-3, 3)$
-2	$4 - 6 + 3 = 1$	$(-2, 1)$
-1	$1 - 3 + 3 = 1$	$(-1, 1)$
0	$0 + 0 + 3 = 3$	$(0, 3)$
1	$1 + 3 + 3 = 7$	$(1, 7)$

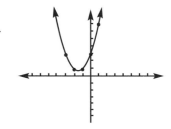

This approach demonstrates that the parabola never touches the x-axis. There are no x-intercepts.

The third method is to use the discriminant of the quadratic equation to count the number of x-intercepts. First, identify the coefficients of each term. The function is $f(x) = x^2 + 3x + 3$. Matching this up to the definition of the standard quadratic equation, $f(x) = ax^2 + bx + c$, we have $a = 1$, $b = 3$, and $c = 3$. Next, write the discriminant from the quadratic formula (the expression that is under the radical sign in the quadratic formula):

$$b^2 - 4ac = 3^2 - 4(1)(3)$$
$$= 9 - 12$$
$$= -3$$

Since the discriminant is less than zero, you cannot take its square root. This means that there is no solution to the equation $f(x) = x^2 + 3x + 3 = 0$, so the function's graph does not touch the x-axis. There are no x-intercepts.

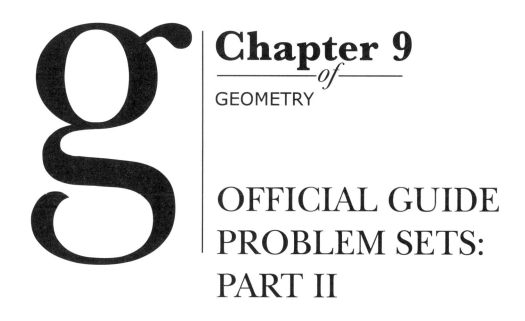

Chapter 9
of
GEOMETRY

OFFICIAL GUIDE
PROBLEM SETS:
PART II

In This Chapter . . .

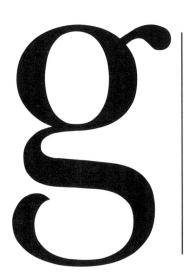

- Geometry Problem Solving List from *The Official Guides:* PART II
- Geometry Data Sufficiency List from *The Official Guides:* PART II

Practicing with REAL GMAT Problems

Now that you have completed Part II of GEOMETRY, it is time to test your skills on problems that have actually appeared on real GMAT exams over the past several years.

The problem sets that follow are composed of questions from three books published by the Graduate Management Admission Council® (the organization that develops the official GMAT exam):

The Official Guide for GMAT Review, 12th Edition
The Official Guide for GMAT Quantitative Review
The Official Guide for GMAT Quantitative Review, 2nd Edition
Note: The two editions of the Quant Review book largely overlap. Use one OR the other.

These books contain quantitative questions that have appeared on past official GMAT exams. (The questions contained therein are the property of The Graduate Management Admission Council, which is not affiliated in any way with Manhattan GMAT.)

Although the questions in the Official Guides have been "retired" (they will not appear on future official GMAT exams), they are great practice questions.

In order to help you practice effectively, we have categorized every problem in The Official Guides by topic and subtopic. On the following pages, you will find two categorized lists:

(1) **Problem Solving:** Lists MORE DIFFICULT Problem Solving Geometry questions contained in *The Official Guides* and categorizes them by subtopic.

(2) **Data Sufficiency:** Lists MORE DIFFICULT Data Sufficiency Geometry questions contained in *The Official Guides* and categorizes them by subtopic.

Remember that Chapter 7 in Part I of this book contains the first sets of Official Guide problems, which are easier.

Each book in Manhattan GMAT's 8-book strategy series contains its own *Official Guide* lists that pertain to the specific topics taught in that particular book. If you complete all the practice problems contained in the *Official Guide* lists in each of the 8 Manhattan GMAT strategy books, you will have completed every single question published in *The Official Guides*.

Problem Solving: Part II

from *The Official Guide for GMAT Review, 12th Edition* (pages 20–23 & 152–185), *The Official Guide for GMAT Quantitative Review* (pages 62–85), and *The Official Guide for GMAT Quantitative Review, 2nd Edition* (pages 62–86). <u>Note</u>: The two editions of the Quant Review book largely overlap. Use one OR the other.

Solve each of the following problems in a notebook, making sure to demonstrate how you arrived at each answer by showing all of your work and computations. If you get stuck on a problem, look back at the GEOMETRY strategies and content contained in this guide to assist you.

<u>Note</u>: Problem numbers preceded by "D" refer to questions in the Diagnostic Test chapter of *The Official Guide for GMAT Review, 12th Edition* (pages 20–23).

<u>ADVANCED SET – GEOMETRY</u>

This set picks up from where the General Set in Part I leaves off.

Polygons
> *12th Edition*: 134
> *Quantitative Review*: 175 OR *2nd Edition*: 135, 175

Triangles and Diagonals
> *12th Edition*: 177, 205, D19
> *QR 2nd Edition*: 150, 157

Circles and Cylinders
> *12th Edition*: 189, 197, D22
> *Quantitative Review*: 141 OR *2nd Edition*: 141, 145, 153, 162

Lines and Angles
> *12th Edition*: 209

Coordinate Plane
> *12th Edition*: 194, 210, 229

<u>CHALLENGE SHORT SET – GEOMETRY</u>

This set covers Geometry problems from each of the content areas, including both easier and harder problems, but with a focus on harder problems. The Challenge Short Set duplicates problems from the General Set (in Part I) and the Advanced Set above.

> *12th Edition*: 33, 39, 62, 88, 134, 152, 177, 189, 197, 209, 210, 229, D10, D22
> *Quantitative Review*: 123, 139, 175 OR *2nd Edition*: 123, 135, 139, 157, 162, 175

Data Sufficiency: Part II

from *The Official Guide for GMAT Review, 12th Edition* (pages 24–26 & 272–288), *The Official Guide for GMAT Quantitative Review* (pages 149–157), and *The Official Guide for GMAT Quantitative Review, 2nd Edition* (pages 152–163). <u>Note</u>: The two editions of the Quant Review book largely overlap. Use one OR the other.

Solve each of the following problems in a notebook, making sure to demonstrate how you arrived at each answer by showing all of your work and computations. If you get stuck on a problem, look back at the GEOMETRY strategies and content contained in this guide to assist you.

Practice REPHRASING both the questions and the statements by using variables and constructing equations. The majority of data sufficiency problems can be rephrased; however, if you have difficulty rephrasing a problem, try testing numbers to solve it. It is especially important that you familiarize yourself with the directions for data sufficiency problems, and that you memorize the 5 fixed answer choices that accompany all data sufficiency problems.

Note: Problem numbers preceded by "D" refer to questions in the Diagnostic Test chapter of *The Official Guide for GMAT Review, 12th edition* (pages 24–26).

ADVANCED SET – GEOMETRY

This set picks up from where the General Set in Part I leaves off.

Polygons
> *12th Edition*: 135, 148, D48

Triangles and Diagonals
> *12th Edition*: 109, 140, 144, 157, 173
> *Quantitative Review*: 117 OR *2nd Edition*: 123

Circles and Cylinders
> *12th Edition*: 117, 160, D36

Lines and Angles
> *12th Edition*: 132

Coordinate Plane
> *12th Edition*: 121, 149, 164, D39

CHALLENGE SHORT SET – GEOMETRY

This set covers Geometry problems from each of the content areas, including both easier and harder problems, but with a focus on harder problems. The Challenge Short Set duplicates problems from the General Set (in Part I) and the Advanced Set above.
> *12th Edition*: 34, 56, 94, 117, 121, 122, 132, 144, 148, 157, 164, 173, D39, D48
> *Quantitative Review*: 58, 70, 87, 91, 109, 117
> OR *2nd Edition*: 59, 72, 91, 95, 114, 123

mbaMission

Every candidate has a unique story to tell.

We have the creative experience to help you tell yours.

We are **mbaMission**, published authors with elite MBA experience who will work with you one-on-one to craft complete applications that will force the admissions committees to take notice. Benefit from straightforward guidance and personal mentorship as you define your unique attributes and reveal them to the admissions committees via a story only you can tell.

We will guide you through our "Complete Start to Finish Process":

- ☑ Candidate assessment, application strategy and program selection
- ☑ Brainstorming and selection of essay topics
- ☑ Outlining and essay structuring
- ☑ Unlimited essay editing
- ☑ Letter of recommendation advice
- ☑ Resume construction and review
- ☑ Interview preparation, mock interviews and feedback
- ☑ Post-acceptance and scholarship counseling

Monday Morning Essay Tip: Overrepresenting Your Overrepresentation

Many in the MBA application pool—particularly male investment bankers—worry that they are overrepresented. While you cannot change your work history, you can change the way you introduce yourself to admissions committees. Consider the following examples:

Example 1: "As an investment banking analyst at Bank of America, I am responsible for creating Excel models…."
Example 2: "At 5:30 pm, I could rest easy. The deadline for all other offers had passed. At that point, I knew…."

In the first example, the candidate starts off by mistakenly introducing the reader to the very over-representation that he/she should be trying to avoid emphasizing. In the second example, the banker immerses the reader in an unraveling mystery. This keeps the reader intrigued and focused on the applicant's story and actions rather than making the specific job title and responsibilities the center of the text. While each applicant's personal situation is different, every candidate can approach his/her story so as to mitigate the effects of overrepresentation.

To schedule a free consultation and read more than fifty Monday Morning Essay Tips, please visit our website:
www.mbamission.com

Did you know you CANNOT use any paper on the actual GMAT?

When taking the GMAT, you can only use a laminated booklet with a felt-tip pen to take notes and work out problems.

Don't be caught off-guard on test day!

Practice with a **Test Simulation Booklet**

Offered Exclusively By

Manhattan GMAT*

A GMAT Prep Essential!

Only $21.00 USD, and it includes the felt-tip pen

FREE with any Complete Prep Set purchase or any ManhattanGMAT Course

Now Available
Get one today at
www.manhattangmat.com

* GMAT and GMAC are registered trademarks of the Graduate Management Admission Council which neither sponsors nor endorses this product.

Finally, a GMAT® prep guide series that goes beyond the basics.

Fractions, Decimals, & Percents, Fourth Edition
ISBN: 978-0-9824238-2-0
Retail: $26

Equations, Inequalities, & VICs, Fourth Edition
ISBN: 978-0-9824238-1-3
Retail: $26

Number Properties, Fourth Edition
ISBN: 978-0-9824238-4-4
Retail: $26

Word Translations, Fourth Edition
ISBN: 978-0-9824238-7-5
Retail: $26

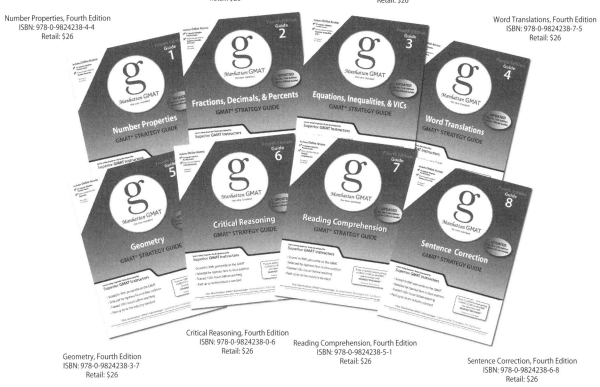

Geometry, Fourth Edition
ISBN: 978-0-9824238-3-7
Retail: $26

Critical Reasoning, Fourth Edition
ISBN: 978-0-9824238-0-6
Retail: $26

Reading Comprehension, Fourth Edition
ISBN: 978-0-9824238-5-1
Retail: $26

Sentence Correction, Fourth Edition
ISBN: 978-0-9824238-6-8
Retail: $26

Published by

Manhattan GMAT

 You get many more pages per topic than you find in all-in-one tomes.

 Only buy those guides that address the specific skills you need to develop.

 Gain access to Online Practice GMAT Exams & Bonus Question Banks.

COMMENTS FROM GMAT TEST TAKERS:

Now Available at your local bookstore!

"Bravo, Manhattan GMAT! Bravo! The guides truly did not disappoint. All the guides are clear, concise, and well organized, and explained things in a manner that made it possible to understand things the first time through without missing any of the important details."

"I've thumbed through a lot of books that don't even touch these. The fact that they're split up into components is immeasurably helpful. The set-up of each guide and the lists of past GMAT problems make for an incredibly thorough and easy-to-follow study path."

GMAT and GMAC are registered trademarks of the Graduate Management Admission Council which neither sponsors nor endorses this product.